NEW ROOTS

EMPOWERING MIGRANT COMMUNITIES FOR GROWTH

A COMMUNITY DEVELOPMENT HANDBOOK

Community Based Strategies for the CALD
(Culturally and Linguistically Diverse)
Communities in Western Australia

Pasan Ganegama

The publisher wishes to acknowledge and thank Dr. Douglas H. Johnson for his invaluable help and support for Africa World Books and its mission of preserving and promoting African cultural and literary traditions and history. Dr. Johnson and fellow historians have been instrumental in ensuring that African people remain connected to their past and their identity. Africa World Books is proud to carry on this mission.

All rights reserved. It is illegal to reproduce, duplicate or transmit any part of this book in either electronic means or printed format. Recording of this publication is strictly prohibited. No part of this publication may be reproduced, stored in a retrieval system, or transmitted, in any form, or by any means, electronic, mechanical, photocopying, recording or otherwise, without the prior permission of the publishers.

Copyright © 2025 Pasan Ganegama

ISBN: 9781763683990

For tertiary students / Community development / Community organization / Social service – Citizen participation

Every effort has been made to trace and acknowledge copyright. However, should any infringement have occurred, the publisher tenders their apologies and invite copyright owner to contact them.

This book is sold subject to the conditions that it shall not, by way of trade or otherwise, be lent, re-sold, hired out or otherwise circulated without the publisher's prior consent in any form of binding or cover other than in which it is published and without a similar condition including the condition being imposed on the subsequent purchaser.

Proofreader: Kanthi Fernando
Cover Design by Mola Senevirathne
Typesetting and layout: Africa World Books
Unit 3, 57 Frobisher St, Osborne Park, WA 6017
P.O. Box 1106 Osborne Park, WA 6916

ABOUT THE AUTHOR

Research Analyst, Cultural Catalyst, Creativity Evangelist—**Pasan Ganegama** embodies the essence of dedication and excellence within Australian public service. His illustrious career, marked by a profound commitment to community development and public welfare, shines as a testament to his unwavering integrity and passion. Currently, Pasan navigates the complexities of insolvencies both individual and coroporates at the Australian Taxation Office with exemplary precision, upholding the highest legislative standards. His pivotal role as a Senate Assurance Tester at the Australian Electoral Commission underscored his critical contribution to safeguarding electoral integrity through meticulous system validation.

Pasan's tenure as a Community Field Officer with the Australian Bureau of Statistics highlighted his exceptional capacity to handle sensitive data with the utmost confidentiality and respect. His educational background including a Bachelor's degree in business management from Sheffield Hallam University and ongoing studies for a Bachelor of Laws at Murdoch University, reflects his dedication to continuous professional growth. Enhanced by specialized training in leadership, cybersecurity, and transfer pricing, his expertise is both broad and profound.

*With Hon. Tony Buti –
Minister for Citizenship & Multicultural Interests*

Honoured with the Australia Day Awards in 2022 and recognized as a finalist for the Multicultural Awards – Western Australia, Pasan's impact extends far beyond conventional roles.

As a published author and the visionary behind a writers' group for migrant adults, he has significantly advanced the voices of Culturally and Linguistically Diverse communities.

His initiative provides a secure and nurturing environment for creative expression, allowing individuals to share their poetry, prose, and stories in their native languages.

Pasan Ganegama's distinguished career and exceptional contributions underscore his remarkable professionalism and profound influence on Australian society, positioning him as a paragon of service, dedication, and innovation.

NEW ROOTS

With CaLD representatives at the OMI Awards, 2021

The cover design, by Mola Senevirathna, is a representation of transformative exploration into the art of building vibrant, inclusive communities from a mosaic of diverse migrant backgrounds. New Roots: Empowering Migrant Communities for Growth provides invaluable insights and actionable strategies for creating inclusive, resilient communities where all member's contributions are valued and celebrated.

TABLE OF CONTENTS

About the Author   iii
Acknowledgement   xiii
Preface   xvii

Part 1 - Understanding communities   1
Chapter 1- What is a 'Community'   3
1.1. Introduction   3
1.2. Community definition   4
1.3. The elements of the community   9
1.4. Summary   13

Chapter 2 - Community capacity   16
2.1. Introduction   16
2.2. Community – Unique factor   18
2.3. Community Strength   23
2.4. Social factors   29
2.5. Assessing Community capacity   31
2.5. Summary   38

Chapter 3: CaLD (Culturally and Linguistically Diverse) Perspective — 41
3.1. Introduction — 41
3.2. CaLD Cultural Perspective — 47
3.3. Working with CaLD communities — 50
3.4. Summary — 54

Part 2: Working with communities — 57
Chapter 4: Community - Concepts and Literature — 59
4.1. Introduction — 59
4.2. Four conceptual approaches — 60
4.3. Defining Terms — 63
4.4. Relationships – The threads that weave through communities — 69
4.5. Reflections and practical work sheets — 76
4.6. Summary — 111

Chapter 5 - Framework for working with communities — 114
5.1. Introduction — 114
5.2. Participative democracy — 119
5.3. Practice framework for integrative partnerships — 122
5.4. Roles – Getting it clear — 131
5.5. Summary — 134

Chapter 6 - Government and Community partnerships   **137**
6.1. Introduction   137
6.1. Australian Government structure   138
6.2. Government roles and modes of state response to community participation   141
6.4. Community engagement – Responsive government policy and practice   145
6.5. Summary   148

Part 3 - Skills in working with communities – CaLD perspective   **151**
Chapter 7 - Community decision making   **153**
7.1. Introduction   155
7.2. Challenges of participative decision making   157
7.3. Hierarchy and Organizational structure for decision making   160
7.4. Key decision-making principles in CaLD communities   163
7.5. Responsibility and community ownership   167
7.6. Summary   169

Chapter 8 - Community partnerships   **183**
8.1. Introduction   184
8.2. Terms and definitions   187
8.3. Effective partnership   188
8.4. Partnership types and development   192
8.5 Summary   195

Chapter 9 - Community planning — **199**
9.1. Introduction — 201
9.2. Social Justice and Human rights perspective — 204
9.3. A Community profile — 208
9.4. Techniques for community planning — 212
9.5. Summary — 224

Chapter 10 - Leading with spirit
– Energy, Leadership and Empowerment — **227**
10.1. Introduction — 229
10.2. Community leadership — 232
10.3. The pace of development — 234
10.4. Competencies — 236
10.5. Practice, theory and application — 240
10.6 Summary — 242

Part 4 - Building knowledge, skills and other competencies — **245**
Chapter 11 - Holistic approach in competencies — **248**
11.1. Introduction — 248
11.2. Community facilitative roles and skills — 250
11.3. Community representational roles and skills — 253
11.4. Community development skills — 255
11.5. Community values and ethics — 258
11.6. Creating support networks — 261
11.7. Summary — 264

Chapter 12 - Helpful Resources   **267**
12.1. Introduction   267
12.1. Resources and available free courses   269
12.2. Summary   272
12.4. Conclusion   274

References   **279**
Index   **287**

Figures
Figure 1- Societal Parameters   6
Figure 2 - Assessing community strength   26
Figure 3 - Community questionnaire sample   32
Figure 4 - Community mapping   33
Figure 5 - Individual with in the larger community   66
Figure 6 - Sample practical work sheets   79
Figure 7 - Piggot- Irvine's action research model   130
Figure 8 - Community service development (CSD)   144
Figure 9 - Analysing engagement process   146
Figure 10 - Smart Organization   161
Figure 11- Structure and decision making models   163
Figure 12 -Communities partnership framework   172
Figure 13 - News article - Examiner newspaper - Feb 17, 2023   175
Figure 14 -Media Statement - 5 Dec 2023   176
Figure 15 - Organisation of African communities in WA   177
Figure 16 - Reflecting the community aspirations   179
Figure 17 -Relationship Types   186

Figure 18 - Partnership life cycle   190
Figure 19 - Partnership Analysis checklist   197
Figure 20 - Expertise in integration
and implementation   231
Figure 21 - Community leadership   233
Figure 22 - Community workpractice roles   252
Figure 23 - Community Development Chain   269

ACKNOWLEDGEMENT

In retrospect, this book has been a major project in my life. Migrant communities and the integration have always inspired my way of thinking about the wider Australian societal tapestry. The context-specific community well-being and community character and the differences that brings with yearly committee changes was amusing and exciting. My basic intention was to write a book encompassing the locally oriented collective actions and the multicultural rhetoric, once the book started to evolve it expanded community partnerships, community leadership and building knowledge. In that context the developmental strategies and the capacity building affects into local communities are being compressed into this book.

Although there are several thousands of community development books, I have targeted this book towards migrant communities. This will help them to define a proper strategy when engaging with sustainable long-term community engagements. This book has no magic formulas but target specifically on blended collective groups of people. Guterbock (1992, p.92)[1] defines community

---

[1] Guterbock TM. Community of interest: Its definition, measurement, and assessment. Sociological Practice Review. 1999;1(2):88-104.

interest as; 'groups of people where there are interactions and a degree of integration because of economic, social, political and/or cultural connections and similarities between people'. Most community development books were written from an academic perspective rather than from the viewpoint of practitioners—those actively engaged in the field of community development. They are predominantly from government, private sector or academia. In that specific context they assume that the reader to have some familiarity with basic social and political ideas or systemic learning at least in first year university level study in areas of sociology, anthropology, politics or other social science disciplines. There are no linear solutions to complex community development problems, as mentioned in academic texts; however, these texts can serve as guideposts. Therefore, it is evident that there is a void in literature for people who do not have that specific qualifications, knowledge, skills and competencies. Of course, for a refugee or a migrant from a war-torn country could not have that specific skill set but have the enthusiasm, energy and zest to do work for the betterment in their communities, where people struggle their newly acquainted systems in the migrated countries. This book target those potential readers and the academia alike.

This book was compiled with the perspective from the communities rather than the academic narrative. The central theme was to present the community aspirations, the way the community is trying to see things in this volatile, uncertain, complex and uncertain social settings. To every person who works tirelessly to uplift and support their community out of sheer love and commitment, I extend my deepest gratitude. Your efforts create ripples of positive change that extend far beyond what can be measured or quantified.

This book stands as a testament to your invaluable work and the profound impact you have on shaping more inclusive, resilient communities. Thank you for all that you do.

Special thanks to Hon. Tony Buti – Minister for Citizenship and Multicultural Interests and for the esteemed community leaders for having long and vigorous conversations in community engagements, during cultural festivities and in coffee shops, including Franco Smargiassi, Nirmal Singh, Dinu Ekanayake, Anuruddha Liyanage, Pille Repnau, Dianne Blanchard and Thanarooban Thanabalasingham for helping to develop the concepts on which this book is built. More recently a special mention to my work colleagues at the Australian Taxation Office, particularly Dennise Mattaboni, Roxanne Nolan, Naomi Summers, Sabina Bhasin, Anjali Chopra, Davidson Almeida, Shawn Fernandez and Gary Foxbridge for their emotional support and encouragement.

As I conclude New Roots: Empowering Migrant Communities for Growth, I am profoundly grateful to those whose expertise and support have been instrumental in bringing this book to fruition.

I would like to extend my sincere gratitude to Mola Senevirathna for crafting such an exceptional cover design for this book. Your ability to capture the essence of community development so vividly and thoughtfully is truly remarkable. The cover not only visually represents the heart of the book but also invites readers into its spirit. Thank you for your creativity and dedication in bringing this project to life and to my proofreader Kanthi Fernando, thank you for your meticulous eye and thorough review. Your careful examination ensured that the final manuscript is free of errors and inconsistencies, allowing the book to reflect the highest standards of accuracy and professionalism.

To the entire publishing team at Africa World Books and specially Peter Deng, your support has been crucial throughout this journey. From the initial concept to the final publication, your collective efforts in design, production, and distribution have brought *'New Roots'* to life. I am grateful for your expertise and dedication, which have made this project a reality.

This book is a testament to your hard work and collaboration, and I am truly thankful for each of your contributions.

But it is my family that really made it possible for this book to see the light of day, and I am indebted to my wife -Dilini Kariyawasam and my son Menuka Ganegama. This book is as much a reflection of their love and support as it is of my own efforts. To my family, your sacrifices and encouragement have been instrumental in making this dream a reality. Thank you for being my rock and my inspiration.

Pasan Ganegama – 2024, Perth, Australia

PREFACE

The disconnection between rhetoric and resources when it comes to community engagement and capacity building is a common issue faced in various fields. While there may be recognition of the importance of these practices, the actual allocation of resources and provision of information to support them can often fall short. This disparity can hinder effective community development and limit the potential impact of initiatives. This book comprised of academic literature and practical insights. The importance of engaging communities and building community capacity is not always matched with resources and information that would support this endeavour.

In this book, I tried to highlight this discrepancy and discuss potential reasons for it. Here are a few factors that contribute to this mismatch:

Limited funding: Many community engagement efforts rely on external funding sources, such as government grants or philanthropic organizations. However, these resources are often insufficient or highly competitive, making it challenging for all communities to access adequate funding for capacity building.

Lack of knowledge transfer: Academics and practitioners may emphasize the importance of community engagement and capacity building in their rhetoric, but there can be a gap in effectively transferring knowledge and providing practical guidance to communities. This could be due to a lack of accessible materials or ineffective dissemination strategies.

Institutional barriers: Organizations and institutions responsible for allocating resources may have bureaucratic processes, rigid funding criteria, or a lack of understanding of community needs. These barriers can impede the flow of resources and information necessary for effective community engagement and capacity building.

Power dynamics and representation: Community engagement should ideally involve meaningful participation from community members and stakeholders. However, power imbalances and unequal representation can hinder the inclusion of marginalized groups or those with limited resources. As a result, their needs may not be adequately addressed in terms of resources and information.

In this book, I have explored strategies to bridge the gap between rhetoric and resources. This includes advocating for cost-effective funding for community initiatives, promoting knowledge transfer through accessible resources and capacity-building programs, and addressing institutional barriers and power imbalances. Additionally, highlighting successful case studies and best practices that can inspire and guide readers in their own efforts to engage communities and build their capacity effectively.

The flow pattern and plan devised on the book

For the easy reference, this book is divided into three separate parts but with a common theme to bind them in a cohesive, integrated spectrum of knowledge. This includes

- Academic theories and concepts related to and relevant to understanding communities

- The approaches of conceptual and practice frameworks that can be used in practical community development strategy
- Knowledge, skills and expertise in working with communities

Part 1: What is your community – Better understand your community.

Chapter One presents a perspective to understand your community. As *Fons Trompenaars* mentions in cross cultural communication, the communities are like 'onions' and have to peel the layers to get into the crux of values. The core principles that is essential to understand community development are,

i. Relationships and partnerships
ii. In-depth understanding of values, beliefs and integration of new and old knowledge (specially related to migrant communities)

It is through a shared understanding and using empathy and tact along with the purposive and goal oriented working relationships will increase the harmony with in community members and wellbeing of community as a whole occurs.

Understanding different communities by using theories and concepts in explained in Chapter 2. Due consideration was given viewing the community development as a 'sequence of interactions'. Then as a 'method' as means to an end subsequently. The theoretical approaches presented are 'Community interaction theory developed by Wilkinson[2] & Sharp[3] (1991) and the social

---

[2] Wilkinson, K. (1991). The community in rural America. New York: Greenwood Press.

[3] Sharp, J. (2001). Locating the Community Field: A study of interorganizational network structure and capacity for community action. Rural Sociology, 66(3), 403-424.

field theory by Kaufman[4] (The community as a social field), to identify, explore and integrate community structures, community elements and processes to improve the capabilities with in the community. The multi-dimensional approach to community development and critique regarding the stratification and less integration is also evaluated.

In Chapter 3, The CaLD (Culturally and Liguistically Diverse) understanding of community is explored. Considering the context of 6000-year-old Australian Aboriginal culture and it's understanding of the community and its relationship to land and water is also very different to the Western understanding. A lot to be done to bridge the gap between the orient and the West (Western Australia)

Part 2: Working with communities

In Chapter 4, The conceptual approaches in capacity building are evaluated. The main focus is on capacity before service. Then the developmental approaches focusing on people rather than programs were elaborated.

Chapter 5 forms a typology of approaches in working with communities. The broader term of participative democracy is used to enhance the 'community empowerment' and the 'developmental' approaches.

Chapter 6 is used to explain the government approaches to work with communities but it is not to gauge or measure the outcomes. The measurement matrix should include different evaluative frameworks and it is yet to be agreed by the communities and different

---

[4] Kaufman, H. F. 1959. Toward an interactional conception of community. Social Forces 38(1):8–17.

stakeholders. Although said it is extremely difficult task as different communities have different aspirations and outcomes.

Part 3: Skills in working with communities
Considerable thought was given to this chapter as this part includes soft skills and emotional intelligence needed to negotiate and agree on common values with in communities. In that context the skills iterated in this chapter are interrelated and generic across all disciplines and useful for both practitioners and wider community members. The following chapters outline a specific skill set that can be harnessed and utilized.

Chapter 7 – Community decision making. The diasporic interventions related to decisions regarding national interests, cultural issues and mitigating factors to integrate rather than segregate.

Chapter 8 – Community partnerships. Effective partnerships with in different ethical and cultural groups with in the community are discussed to enhance collaboration.

Chapter 9 – Effective Community planning. Special emphasis on social justice and human rights perspective as it is an incumbent factor when it comes to the community profile. The profiling is complemented with community planning techniques

Chapter 10 – Leading with spirit – Leadership, Energy and Empowerment. Community work is rewarding in the long term and in short term it takes effort and dedication. If only engaged in community development for short-term goals it will not be a pleasurable experience. To keep abreast with the societal changes and to seek avenues to maximize the effects for the betterment of the community needs commitment and to mitigate the adverse effects from the societal changes the practitioner/ community member should have proper strategies in place. Several back-up plans to counter the effects specific to the community is also needed. These are addressed in 'pace of development' and 'practice, theory and application' parts in the chapter.

Part 4: Building knowledge, skills and other competencies
Chapter 11 – Holistic approach in competencies - This chapter is used to illustrate principles, approaches and best practices in working with communities. There is no one specific 'right answer' to all the community development strategies. The approaches vary depending on the specific community, the community members values and experiences and their short-term and long term community expectations.

Chapter 12 – Helpful resources. The free courses offered by the 'Office of Multicultural Interests' – 'OMI' and other relevant websites are presented.

All the resources reflect the general principles involved in working with communities rather than a particular discipline specific approach and I suggest that there is no 'one right way, and that people's approaches will be influenced by their discipline, their values and experiences. By integrating people's experiences with the concepts and practical skills presented in this book, the outcome will be of most value in learning about working with communities. Websites are listed at the end of each chapter and provide practical information about the topics discussed in each chapter.

PART ONE

UNDERSTANDING COMMUNITIES

Chapter One introduces the notion of 'Community' and the importance of it in the contemporary context.

Chapter two provides consideration viewing the community development as a 'sequence of interactions'. Then as a 'method' as means to an end subsequently. The theoretical approaches presented are 'Community interaction theory developed by Wilkinson[5] & Sharp[6] (1991) and the Social field theory by Kaufman[7] (The community as a social field), to identify, explore and integrate community structures, community elements and processes to improve the

---

5 Wilkinson, K. (1991). The community in rural America. New York: Greenwood Press.

6 Sharp, J. (2001). Locating the Community Field: A study of interorganizational network structure and capacity for community action. Rural Sociology, 66(3), 403-424.

7 Kaufman, H. F. 1959. Toward an interactional conception of community. Social Forces 38(1):8–17.

capabilities with in the community. The multi-dimensional approach to community development and critique regarding the stratification and less integration is also evaluated.

Chapter three, The CaLD (Culturally and Linguistically Diverse) understanding of community is explored. Considering the 6000 year old Australian Aboriginal culture and it's understanding of the community and its relationship to land and water is also very different to the Western understanding. This gap was not addressed during the past decades by the policy makers and the community leaders. We can take insights and considerable thought from this disconnect to better include soft skills and emotional intelligence required to negotiate and agree on common values within communities.

CHAPTER 1

COMMUNITY: THE PARADIGM SHIFT FROM TRADITIONAL TO ELECTRONIC PERSPECTIVE

1.1. Introduction

This chapter will:
- Define the traditional terminology, in respect to traditional perspective and the differentiation in modern electronic era;
- Explain why the principles of community development underpins healthy societies and social care developments;
- Importance in understanding communities.
- Significance of partnerships between communities, practitioners, organizations, governments and funding agencies to create sustainable organic growth in communities.

What is a 'Community'

A community is a social unit with commonality such as place, norms, religion, values, customs, or identity. Communities may share a sense of place situated in a given geographical area (e.g. a country, village, town, or neighbourhood) or in virtual space through communication platforms. Durable good relations that extend beyond immediate genealogical ties also define a sense of community, important to their identity, practice, and roles in social institutions such as family, home, work, government, society, or humanity at large.

1.2 Community definition

Here are some examples of different types of communities:

Geographic communities are groups of people who live in the same area. This could be a neighbourhood, town, city, or even a country. Interest communities are groups of people who share a common interest or passion. This could be anything from a sports team to a book club to a political group. Action communities are groups of people who are working together to achieve a common goal. This could be anything from cleaning up a local park to starting a new business. In this context, for this chapter, I have drawn heavily upon the concept of 'community' as both a theoretical and practical framework. My exploration into community development is deeply informed by academic perspectives that underscore the multifaceted nature of what it means to belong and contribute to a collective.

Community, as discussed in the works of scholars such as Benedict Anderson (1983) in *Imagined Communities*[8] and Robert Putnam (2000) in *Bowling Alone*[9], is not merely a collection of

---

8 Anderson, B. (2016). *Imagined communities*. Verso Books.

9 Putnam, R. D. (2000). Bowling alone: the collapse and revival of American community. New York, Simon & Schuster.

individuals but a dynamic and interconnected fabric of relationships and shared values. Anderson's notion of 'imagined communities' highlights the role of shared identities and collective aspirations in forming cohesive groups, while Putnam's research emphasizes the importance of social capital and civic engagement in strengthening community bonds.

These theoretical insights have guided my examination of how migrant communities can be effectively developed and supported. The chapter integrates these academic perspectives with practical strategies, demonstrating how diverse cultural elements can contribute to a richer, more inclusive community experience. Virtual communities are groups of people who interact online. This could be through social media, forums, or even video games. No matter what type of community it is, all communities share some common characteristics. These include:

- A sense of belonging
- A sense of shared values
- A sense of shared goals
- A sense of mutual support

Communities can provide a number of benefits to their members. These benefits can include:

- A sense of belonging and identity
- Social support
- A sense of purpose
- A sense of security
- Access to resources and opportunities

Figure 1 - Societal Parameters

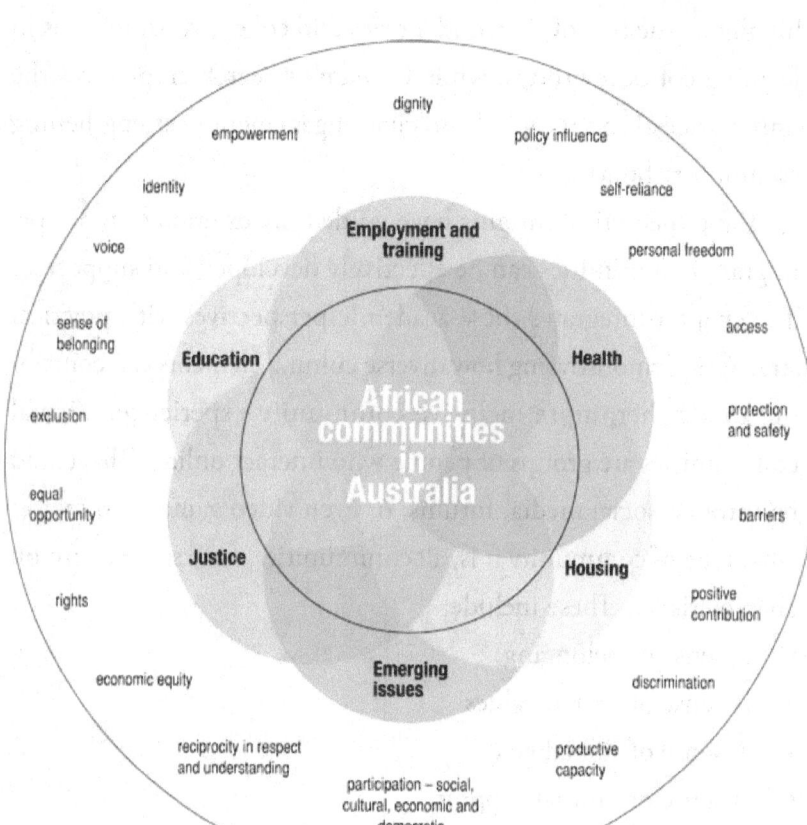

Societal Parameters – 'Extracted from – Australian Human Rights commission report - Discussion Paper: African Australians: A report on human rights and social inclusion issues (2009)[10]"

Communities can also play a role in shaping the individual and collective identities of their members. They can provide a sense

---

10 https://humanrights.gov.au/our-work/discussion-paper-african-australians-report-human-rights-and-social-inclusion-issues-2009

of belonging, a sense of shared values, and a sense of purpose. Communities can also provide social support and access to resources and opportunities.

In today's world, it is more important than ever to be part of a community. Communities can provide us with the support and resources we need to thrive. They can also help us to feel connected to something larger than ourselves.

1.2.1. Academic definitions

Academic definitions of "community" are diverse and often depend on the specific discipline or theoretical framework. However, several key themes emerge:
- Interaction and social ties: Communities involve individuals who interact and form social bonds, whether through shared interests, location, or experiences.
- Shared perspectives and identities: Members often share a sense of belonging, identity, or common ground, based on values, goals, or cultural practices.
- Joint action and collaboration: Communities may engage in collective activities or work towards shared goals, fostering cooperation and collaboration.

Different perspectives:
- Place-based communities: Focus on geographic proximity and shared space, such as neighbourhoods, villages, or cities.
- Communities of interest: Emphasize shared interests, activities, or goals, such as professional networks, hobby groups, or online communities.
- Communities of identity: Highlight shared characteristics like

ethnicity, religion, or social class, creating a sense of belonging and solidarity.

Critical perspectives:
Power dynamics and inequalities: Recognize that communities can be shaped by power imbalances and social inequalities, leading to exclusion and marginalization of certain groups.

Fluidity and dynamism: Emphasize the fluid and dynamic nature of communities, recognizing how they evolve over time and can be contested or reimagined.

Here are some examples of academic definitions:

a. Sociology: "A group of people who live in the same locality and share common interests or characteristics." (Robert Stebbins[11])
b. Anthropology: "A collection of people who share a common territory and meet their basic physical and social needs through daily interaction with one another." (Allan Johnson[12])
c. Communication Studies: "A group of individuals who share common interests, goals, and symbols and who interact with one another through a variety of channels." (John Fiske[13])
d. Public Health: "A group of people with diverse characteristics who are linked by social ties, share common perspectives, and engage in joint action in geographic locations or settings." (National Institutes of Health[14])

---

11 Robert Stebbins, *Sociology. The Study of Society*, Harper and Row: New York, 1987, p. 534).

12 Allan Johnson, *Human Arrangements*, Harcourt Brace Jovanovich Publishers: Orlando, 1986, p. 692).

13 Fiske, J. (2010). Introduction to communication studies. Routledge.

14 MacQueen, K. M., McLellan, E., Metzger, D. S., Kegeles, S., Strauss, R. P.,

Ultimately, the "right" definition of community depends on the specific context and purpose. As you explore different definitions, consider the specific characteristics, dynamics, and challenges relevant to the community you are interested in.

1.3. The elements of the community

The elements of community structure and functions can vary depending on the specific community. However, some common elements include:

i. Structure Members: The community is made up of individuals who share common characteristics, such as geography, interests, or values.
ii. Relationships: The members of the community interact with each other in a variety of ways, such as face-to-face, online, or through other forms of communication.
iii. Leadership: The community may have formal or informal leaders who help to coordinate the activities of the community and to represent the community to the outside world.
iv. Institutions: The community may have institutions, such as schools, businesses, or religious organizations, which provide services to the community and help to promote its goals.

1.3.1. Essential or expected functions:

a. Providing social support: The community can provide its members with social support, such as emotional support, practical help, and companionship.

Scotti, R., Blanchard, L., & Trotter, R. T., 2nd (2001). What is community? An evidence-based definition for participatory public health. *American journal of public health*, *91*(12), 1929–1938.

b. Promoting social cohesion: The community can promote social cohesion, which is the sense of belonging and connection that people feel to their community.
c. Generating social capital: The community can generate social capital, which is the networks of relationships and trust that exist within the community.
d. Achieving common goals: The community can work together to achieve common goals, such as improving the quality of life, promoting social justice, or protecting the environment.

In short, the elements of community structure and functions can vary depending on the specific community. However, all communities share the common goal of providing their members with a sense of belonging, support, and connection.

1.3.2. Why work/engage with communities

1.3.2.1. Links between community, health and well-being

A sense of belonging: A sense of belonging is one of the most important factors for health and wellbeing. When people feel like they belong to a community, they are more likely to be happy, healthy, and engaged in their lives.

a. Social support: Communities can provide social support, which is the help and assistance that people receive from others. Social support can help people to cope with stress, manage their health, and achieve their goals.
b. Access to resources: Communities can provide access to resources, such as healthcare, education, and employment opportunities. These resources can help people to improve their health and wellbeing.

c. A sense of purpose: Communities can provide a sense of purpose, which is a feeling of meaning and direction in life. When people feel like they are part of something bigger than themselves, they are more likely to be happy and healthy.

There is a growing body of evidence that shows that communities can play a significant role in improving health and wellbeing. For example, a study published in the journal Social Science & Medicine found that people who live in communities with a strong sense of social cohesion are more likely to report good health and wellbeing.

1.3.2.2. There are several ways to strengthen the links between community, health, and wellbeing:

a. Support community-based organizations: Community-based organizations play a vital role in providing social support, resources, and opportunities to community members. Supporting CBOs can help to strengthen communities and improve the health and wellbeing of their members.

b. Encourage civic engagement: Civic engagement is the involvement of citizens in the political and social life of their community. Civic engagement can help to build stronger communities and improve the health and wellbeing of their members.

c. Create safe and supportive environments: Safe and supportive environments are essential for health and wellbeing. Communities can create safe and supportive environments by investing in parks, recreation centres, and other community amenities.

d. Promote social cohesion: Social cohesion is the sense of

connection and belonging that people feel to their community. Promoting social cohesion can help to improve health and wellbeing by reducing stress, isolation, and loneliness.

By strengthening the links between community, health, and wellbeing, we can create healthier and more equitable communities for all.

1.3.3. Principles in working with communities

There are a few principles that should be followed when working with communities. These principles include:

i. Respect: Respect for the community and its members is essential. This means listening to the community, understanding its needs and concerns, and respecting its culture and values.
ii. Participation: Community members should be involved in all aspects of the work, from planning and decision-making to implementation and evaluation. This will help to ensure that the work is relevant and responsive to the needs of the community.
iii. Empowerment: The goal of working with communities is to empower them to act and solve their own problems. This means providing the community with the resources and support they need to be successful.
iv. Sustainability: The work should be designed to be sustainable, meaning that it can be sustained by the community after the external support ends. This can be done by building capacity within the community and by developing long-term partnerships.
v. Accountability: The community should be able to hold the external actors accountable for their work. This can be done through clear and transparent reporting mechanisms and through mechanisms for community feedback.

By following these principles, we can build stronger and more resilient communities. Here are some additional tips for working with communities:

1. Build relationships: Take the time to build relationships with community members. Get to know them, understand their needs, and build trust.
2. Be flexible: Be willing to adapt your plans to the needs of the community. Don't be afraid to change course if necessary.
3. Be patient: It takes time to build strong relationships and to create change. Be patient and persistent.
4. Celebrate successes: When there are successes, be sure to celebrate them. This will help to build momentum and motivation.

By following these tips, you can increase the chances of success when working with communities.

1.4. Summary

A community is a social unit characterized by shared attributes such as location, norms, religion, values, customs, or identity. Communities can be defined by geographical areas, like neighbourhood's or towns, or virtual spaces, such as online forums. They are marked by enduring relationships and a collective identity that extends beyond immediate genealogical ties, impacting roles in various social institutions. Types of communities include geographic ones based on shared location, interest-based groups united by common passions, action-oriented groups working towards specific goals, and virtual communities interacting online.

Academic perspectives emphasize that communities are not merely collections of individuals but dynamic networks of relationships and shared values. For instance, Benedict Anderson's concept of "imagined communities" and Robert Putnam's focus on social capital illustrate how identity and civic engagement shape community cohesion. Essential elements of communities include their structure, relationships, leadership, and institutions, which collectively provide social support, promote cohesion, and work towards common goals. Engaging with communities fosters a sense of belonging, purpose, and access to resources, which are crucial for individual and collective well-being. Principles of respect, participation, empowerment, sustainability, and accountability guide effective community work.

Useful Websites

For those engaged in community development within Australia, several local websites provide essential resources, support, and information tailored to Australian contexts. Here are some key websites that can enhance your community development efforts:

1. Australian Community Workers Association (ACWA): www.acwa.org.au ACWA offers resources, professional development opportunities, and advocacy for community workers across Australia. Their website includes information on best practices, industry standards, and educational resources.

2. Community Arts Network (CAN): www.can.org.au CAN focuses on the role of arts in community development. Their site provides access to case studies, project examples, and resources that demonstrate how community arts initiatives can foster social change and engagement.

3. The Foundation for Rural & Regional Renewal (FRRR): www.frrr.org.au FRRR supports rural and regional communities through grants and resources. Their website offers information on funding opportunities, community success stories, and resources to support local development projects.

5. Australian Council of Social Service (ACOSS): www.acoss.org.au ACOSS is a leading advocate for social justice in Australia. Their website includes policy research, advocacy tools, and resources that address issues of social inclusion and community well-being.

These websites provide critical tools and information for community development professionals in Australia. By utilizing these resources, practitioners can stay informed, enhance their skills, and effectively contribute to building vibrant and resilient communities across the nation.

CHAPTER 2

COMMUNITY CAPACITY

2.1. Introduction

This chapter aims to:

- Simplify the concepts that helps to understand community capacity, including the community strength, entrepreneurial social infrastructure and social capital;
- Identify and define community capacity with special insights to CaLD communities; and
- Give an academic perspective enabling practitioners and communities to assess community capacity

This chapter delves into the crucial role of community social capacities in promoting both individual and collective health and well-being, driving social and economic development, and addressing local challenges. Central to our discussion is the concept of community capacity and its measurement, which serves as a foundation for understanding how communities can effectively mobilize resources and engage in problem-solving activities.

We explore several related concepts to deepen our comprehension of community capacity. These include community strength, as discussed by Black and Hughes (2001[15]) and Cheers et al. (2004[16]), which underscores the intrinsic resilience and resources within communities that contribute to their ability to foster well-being and address issues. Additionally, we examine the notion of entrepreneurial social infrastructure introduced by Flora (1998[17]), highlighting how communities can leverage social networks and local initiatives to stimulate economic development and innovation.

The chapter also engages with the concept of social capital, a framework thoroughly explored by Bordieu (1985[18]), Coleman (1988[19]), Portes (1998[20]), and Putnam (1995[21]). Social capital refers to the networks, norms, and trust that facilitate coordination and cooperation among community members, thereby enhancing their collective capabilities and fostering a supportive environment for growth and problem resolution.

---

15 Black, A. Hughes, P. (2001), *The Identification and analysis of indicators of Community strenghs and outcomes,* Occasional paper No.3., Department of Family and Community Services, Canberra

16 Cheers, B. Edwards, J & Graham, L. (2004) 'Community strength and health in rural communities', Proceedings of the SA PHC_RED Conference, J Fuller (ed.), Adelaide.

17 Flora, J.L. (1998), 'Social capital and communities of place', *Rural Sociology,* Vol.63, no. 4, pp. 481-505.

18 Bordeaux, P. (1985), 'The forms of capital', in J.G Richardson (ed.), *Handbook of Theory and Research for Sociology of Education,* Greenwood, New York, pp.241-58.

19 Coleman, J. (1988), 'Social capital in the creation of human capital', *American Journal of Sociology,* Vol.94, Supplement: s95-s120

20 Portes, A. (1998), "Social Capital: its origins and applications in Modern sociology'. *Annual Review of Sociology,* Vol. 13, pp. 1-24

21 Putnam, R. D. (1993), 'Bowling Alone: America's declining social capital', *Journal of Democracy, vol. 6, pp. 65-78*

By integrating these concepts, we aim to provide a comprehensive understanding of how community capacities can be cultivated and measured to support sustainable development and improve overall quality of life. This analysis offers valuable insights for practitioners, policymakers, and researchers dedicated to strengthening communities and advancing their potential for positive impact.

2.2. Community – Unique factor

We define the community factor as all the capacities a community has that are inherent in how it functions socially. This chapter focuses on the pivotal role of community social capacities in advancing both individual and collective health and well-being, fostering social and economic development, and tackling local issues. Key to this exploration is the evaluation of community capacity and its measurement, providing a framework for understanding how communities can harness their internal resources and address challenges effectively.

A significant aspect of this discussion involves the evaluation of community factors as outlined by Wilkinson (1970[22]). Wilkinson's work provides a foundational perspective on how various community factors—such as social cohesion, collective action, and resource availability—impact a community's capacity to manage and solve its own problems. His evaluation framework emphasizes the importance of assessing these factors to understand how they contribute to community development and overall effectiveness.

In addition to Wilkinson's evaluation framework, the chapter explores related concepts to enrich our understanding of community capacity. We discuss the concept of community strength, drawing on

---

22 Wilkinson, K. (1970). 'The community as a social field', *Social Forces,* Vol. 48, pp. 311-22

the work of Black and Hughes (2001[23]) and Cheers et al. (2004), which highlights the inherent resilience and resourcefulness within communities. Entrepreneurial social infrastructure, as proposed by Flora (1998[24]), is also examined, revealing how communities can leverage local networks and initiatives to drive economic growth and innovation.

Furthermore, the chapter integrates the concept of social capital, as extensively analyzed by Bordieu (1985[25]), Coleman (1988), Portes (1998), and Putnam (1995). Social capital refers to the networks, norms, and trust that facilitate cooperation and collective action, thereby enhancing community capacities and fostering supportive environments for addressing challenges.

By incorporating Wilkinson's evaluation framework alongside these complementary concepts, the chapter aims to offer a nuanced understanding of how community capacities can be assessed and strengthened. This comprehensive analysis provides valuable insights for practitioners, policymakers, and researchers dedicated to enhancing community effectiveness and improving quality of life.

A community factor is a characteristic of a community that can influence its overall well-being. Community factors can be physical, social, economic, or environmental.

Some examples of community factors include:

a. Physical factors: The physical environment of a community can have a significant impact on its residents' health and well-being. For example, communities with high levels of air pollution or crime rates may have lower levels of health and well-being than communities with cleaner air and lower crime rates.

---

23 Ibid 15

24 Ibid 17

25 Ibid 18

b. Social factors: The social fabric of a community can also play a role in its overall well-being. For example, communities with strong social bonds and cohesiveness may have lower levels of crime and violence than communities with weak social bonds and high levels of social isolation.
c. Economic factors: The economic conditions of a community can also have an impact on its residents' well-being. For example, communities with high levels of poverty and unemployment may have lower levels of health and well-being than communities with strong economies and low levels of unemployment.
d. Environmental factors: The environmental conditions of a community can also play a role in its overall well-being. For example, communities with polluted air and water may have higher rates of respiratory illness and other health problems than communities with clean air and water.

Community factors can interact with each other in complex ways. For example, a community with a strong social fabric may be better able to address the challenges of poverty and environmental pollution.

By understanding the community factors that are important to its residents, community leaders can develop strategies to improve the overall well-being of their community.

2.2.1. Community capacities discussion – Generic or purpose specific

In the academic exploration of community capacities, McLean[26], Cheers[27], and Kruger (2007) offer significant insights into whether community capacities are generic or purpose-specific. This distinction is critical for understanding how communities can effectively mobilize their resources and strengths to address various challenges and achieve specific goals.

2.2.1.1. Generic Community Capacities

Generic community capacities refer to the broad, foundational strengths and resources that a community possesses regardless of the specific issue or objective at hand. These capacities are fundamental attributes that underpin a community's overall ability to function and adapt, such as social cohesion, general trust among members, and basic organizational structures. McLean et al. (2007[28]) argue that these capacities are essential for enabling a community to handle diverse challenges, as they provide a baseline of resilience and functionality that can be leveraged in various contexts.

For example, a community with strong generic capacities might have well-established social networks, a high level of civic engagement, and a robust infrastructure of local organizations. These general attributes facilitate the community's ability to mobilize resources, communicate effectively, and engage in collective action

---

26 McLean, R. & Stutter, H. (1993), *Advocacy Training in Community Services:* a Training Package for consumers and service providers, TasCOSS/ Tasmania TAFE

27 Ibid 16

28 Ibid 26

across a range of issues, from public health crises to economic development initiatives.

2.2.1.2. Purpose-Specific Community Capacities

In contrast, purpose-specific community capacities are tailored to particular goals or challenges. These capacities are developed or enhanced in response to specific needs or objectives, such as addressing a local environmental issue, implementing a health intervention, or pursuing economic development projects. McLean et al. (2007[29]) emphasize that purpose-specific capacities involve targeted skills, knowledge, and resources that are designed to achieve particular outcomes.

For instance, a community focusing on environmental sustainability might build purpose-specific capacities in areas such as environmental science, advocacy, and policy development. These targeted skills and resources are crucial for addressing the unique aspects of environmental challenges and achieving specific sustainability goals.

2.2.1.3. The Balance Between Generic and Purpose-Specific Capacities

McLean, Cheers, and Kruger (2007) highlight that while both generic and purpose-specific capacities are important, their interplay is essential for effective community development. Generic capacities provide a solid foundation for any community initiative, facilitating general functioning and adaptability. Purpose-specific capacities, however, enable communities to address particular issues more effectively by applying specialized knowledge and resources.

---

[29] Ibid

In practice, successful community development often involves leveraging both types of capacities. For example, a community might use its generic capacities to build a strong, participatory framework while developing purpose-specific capacities to address a specific problem, such as a public health initiative or an economic development program. By integrating these capacities, communities can enhance their overall effectiveness and achieve more targeted and meaningful outcomes.

In summary, McLean, Cheers, and Kruger (2007[30]) provide a nuanced perspective on community capacities by distinguishing between generic and purpose-specific types. This distinction helps in understanding how communities can optimize their resources and strengths to address diverse challenges and pursue specific objectives effectively.

2.3. Community Strength

Community strength is a complex concept that encompasses a wide range of factors, including the skills and resources of community members, the strength of community bonds, and the ability of the community to work together.

a. Some of the key elements of community strength include:
a) Strong social bonds: A community with strong social bonds is one where people feel a sense of belonging and connection to their neighbours. This can be achieved through activities such as volunteering, attending community events, and simply getting to know your neighbours.
b. A sense of community identity: A community with a strong sense of identity is one where people share a common vision for the future of their community. This can be achieved through

---

[30] Ibid

community events, festivals, and other activities that bring people together.
c. A sense of shared responsibility: A community with a strong sense of shared responsibility is one where people feel a sense of ownership over their community and are willing to work together to solve problems. This can be achieved through community engagement, such as attending town hall meetings and participating in community projects.
d. Access to resources: A community with access to resources is one where people have the tools they need to succeed. This includes access to education, healthcare, employment opportunities, and other essential services.
e. A supportive environment: A community with a supportive environment is one where people feel safe and respected. This can be achieved through programs and policies that promote tolerance and understanding.

Community strength is not something that happens overnight. It takes time, effort, and commitment from all members of the community. However, by working together, communities can build a strong foundation for a thriving future.

Academic perspective on 'Community Strength'
In their 2001 study, Black and Hughes provide a nuanced perspective on the concept of community strength, emphasizing its integral role in fostering effective community development and resilience. They conceptualize community strength as a multifaceted attribute that underpins a community's ability to function cohesively and address its collective needs.

At the heart of their analysis is the idea that community strength is deeply rooted in the quality and nature of social networks and relationships within the community. Black and Hughes argue that the density and quality of these social connections are crucial for enabling communities to mobilize resources, share information, and support one another effectively. Strong social networks facilitate the exchange of support and resources, thus enhancing the community's capacity to act collectively.

Another critical dimension they explore is '**collective efficacy**', which refers to a community's shared belief in its capacity to achieve common goals. High levels of collective efficacy contribute to increased engagement and a collaborative spirit among community members. It reflects the community's confidence in its ability to tackle challenges and work towards shared objectives, thereby reinforcing its overall strength.

Shared values and norms are also emphasized as foundational elements of community strength. Black and Hughes suggest that when community members have common values and norms, it creates a sense of belonging and solidarity. This shared understanding aligns individual actions with broader community goals, fostering cohesion and facilitating coordinated efforts.

The role of leadership and organizational capacity is another significant focus of their discussion. Effective leadership is seen as pivotal in guiding community efforts, mobilizing resources, and implementing strategies. Organizational capacity, including the presence of both formal and informal institutions, supports the community's ability to manage initiatives, deliver services, and achieve its objectives efficiently.

Black and Hughes' perspective highlights that enhancing

community strength involves addressing these dimensions—social networks, collective efficacy, shared values, and leadership. By focusing on these aspects, communities can build resilience, improve their capacity for collective action, and achieve more sustainable development outcomes. Their work underscores the importance of nurturing these attributes to create robust and cohesive communities capable of navigating challenges and seizing opportunities.

Figure 2 - Assessing community strength

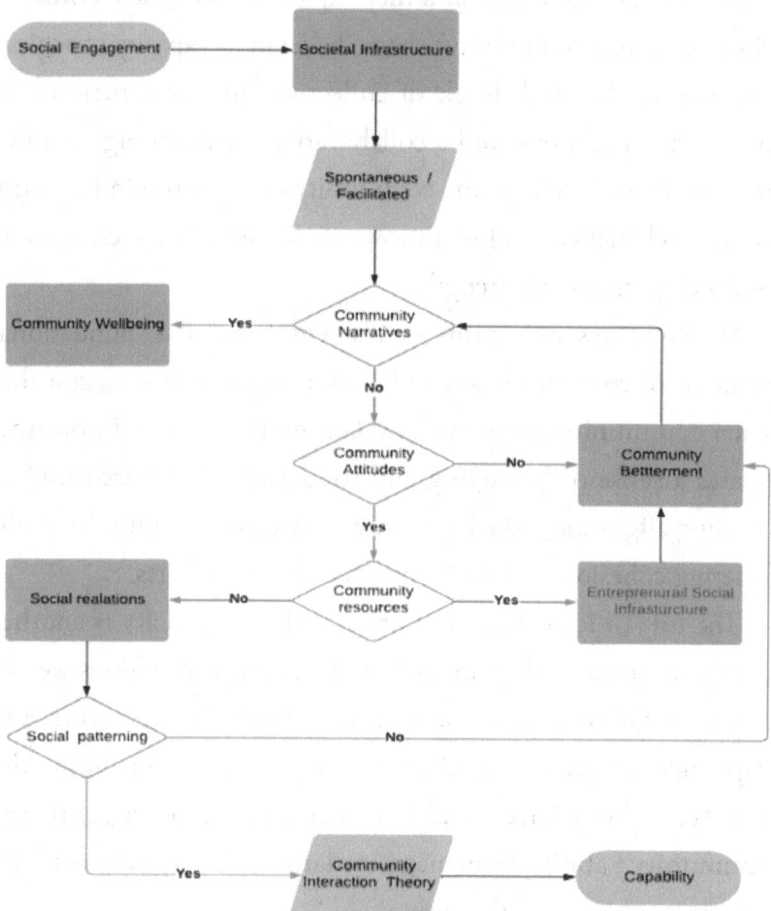

Flow Chart Key: Blue – Terminator / Purple – Process / Green – Data / Red - Decision

In Cheers et al. (2004[31]) offer a nuanced framework for assessing 'community strength,' emphasizing a multi-dimensional approach that incorporates various aspects of community functionality and resilience. This framework integrates concepts from social capital, collective efficacy, resource utilization, leadership, and shared values, providing a comprehensive method for evaluating community capacities.

At the core of their framework is the concept of **social capital**, which refers to the networks of relationships and the level of trust and norms that facilitate cooperation within a community (Putnam, 2000[32]; Coleman, 1988[33]). To assess social capital, Cheers et al. suggest examining the density and quality of these social networks. This involves evaluating the extent of community engagement and the strength of relationships among members. Surveys and interviews that measure levels of trust, reciprocity, and participation in collective activities are essential tools in this assessment process.

Another critical dimension is **collective efficacy**, which is the community's shared belief in its ability to address common problems and achieve collective goals (Sampson et al., 1997[34]). Cheers et al. propose evaluating collective efficacy by investigating community members' perceptions of their capacity to influence outcomes and their involvement in decision-making processes. This can be done through qualitative research methods, such as interviews and focus groups, which explore how confident residents feel about

---

31 Ibid 16

32 Ibid 21

33 Ibid 19

34 *Sampson, R. J., Raudenbush, S. W., & Earls, F. (1997). Neighborhoods and violent crime: A multilevel study of collective efficacy. science, 277(5328), 918-924.*

their collective problem-solving abilities and their participation in local governance.

The availability and effective utilization of **resources** also play a vital role in community strength. Cheers et al. argue that assessing community resources involves mapping out the financial, human, and physical assets within the community and evaluating how these resources are utilized to support development. This assessment might include inventories of local organizations, funding sources, and volunteer networks, as well as analyses of resource allocation and management practices (Flora, 1998).

Leadership and **governance** structures are crucial for fostering community strength, according to Cheers et al. They emphasize the need to assess both formal leadership (e.g., elected officials) and informal leadership (e.g., respected community figures). The quality of leadership and governance can be evaluated through interviews and surveys that explore leadership styles, decision-making processes, and the capacity of governance structures to engage and address community needs (Black & Hughes, 2001[35]).

Finally, shared **values and norms** contribute significantly to community cohesion and collective action. Cheers et al. suggest that understanding the extent to which community members share common values and norms is important for assessing community strength. This can be achieved through qualitative research methods that capture cultural and normative dimensions of community life, such as ethnographic studies and focus groups (Bourdieu, 1985[36]).

In summary, Cheers et al. advocate for a holistic approach to assessing community strength, combining empirical methods to

---

35 Ibid 15

36 Ibid 18

capture social capital, collective efficacy, resource availability, leadership, and shared values. This comprehensive assessment helps identify strengths and areas for development, facilitating more effective community interventions and policies.

Here are some specific examples of how community strength can be used to address community problems:

i. A community with strong social bonds may be better able to address the problem of crime by working together to create a safer environment for everyone.
ii. A community with a strong sense of community identity may be better able to address the problem of poverty by working together to develop economic opportunities for all residents.
iii. A community with a strong sense of shared responsibility may be better able to address the problem of environmental pollution by working together to reduce waste and protect the environment.

Community strength is a powerful force that can be used to address a wide range of community problems. By strengthening the social fabric of their communities, community members can create a more just and equitable society for everyone.

2.4. Social factors

A community social factor is a characteristic of a community that can influence its overall well-being. Community factors can be physical, social, economic, or environmental. Here are some examples of community factors:

a. **Physical factors.** Crime rate: The crime rate in a community can have a significant impact on its residents' sense of safety and well-being. Air quality: The air quality in a community can affect the health of its residents. Access to green space: Green space can provide opportunities for recreation and relaxation, as well as improve air quality.

b. **Social factors.** Sense of community: The sense of community in a neighbourhood can contribute to a sense of belonging and support. Social capital: Social capital is the networks and relationships that people have with each other. It can help people to access resources and support. Volunteerism: Volunteerism can help to build community spirit and improve the quality of life for residents.

c. **Economic factors.** Income level: The income level of a community can affect its residents' access to resources, such as housing, education, and healthcare. Unemployment rate: The unemployment rate in a community can affect its residents' financial well-being. Access to jobs: Access to jobs can help residents to earn a living and support their families.

d. **Environmental factors:** Pollution: Pollution can have a negative impact on the health of residents and the environment. Access to clean water: Access to clean water is essential for human health and well-being. Access to green space: Green space can provide opportunities for recreation and relaxation, as well as improve air quality. Community factors can interact with each other in complex ways. For example, a community with a high crime rate may also have a low sense of community, which can make it more difficult to address the crime problem. By understanding the community factors that are important to its residents, community leaders can develop strategies to improve the overall well-being of their community.

2.5. Assessing Community capacity

Community capacity is the ability of a community to solve its own problems and improve its own well-being. It is a complex concept that encompasses a wide range of factors, including the skills and resources of community members, the strength of community bonds, and the ability of the community to work together. There are many ways to assess community capacity. Some common methods include:

a) Community surveys: Community surveys can be used to gather information about the needs and priorities of community members. This information can be used to identify areas where community capacity needs to be strengthened.

Fig 3. Sample community survey questionnaire

Please indicate which of the following best describes you?			
(If aged under 18, ask if there is a person in the household who is over 18, if not, terminate the interview)			
18 years	1	60 - 74 years	5
20 to 34 years	2	75 years or over	6
35 to 44 years	3	Prefer not to say	9
45 to 59 years	4		

With which gender do you identify?			
Male	1	Other	4
Female	2	Prefer not to say	9

Do you speak a language other than English at home?			
English only	1	Other *(specify):*_____	2

On a scale of 1 (strongly disagree) to 5 (strongly agree), how much do you agree or disagree with each of the following statements?

Statement	Strongly disagree	Disagree	Neutral	Agree	Strongly agree	Can't say
1. This is a close-knit neighbourhood	1	2	3	4	5	9
2. People in this neighbourhood can be trusted	1	2	3	4	5	9
3. People around here are willing to help their neighbours	1	2	3	4	5	9

Community questionnaire sample

Once generic information is obtained more specific questions can be asked to gather priorities. – **'Word of caution' – Inform to get their consent before the questionnaire and data & privacy protection strategies should be in place.**

b) Community forums: Community forums are a way for community members to come together and discuss issues that are important to them. This can help to build relationships and create a sense of shared purpose.

c) Community mapping: Community mapping is a process of identifying and mapping the assets of a community. This can include things like physical resources, community organizations, and social networks. This information can be used to identify areas where community capacity needs to be strengthened and to develop strategies for improving the community.

Fig 4. Community Mapping

1. Define the community: (Remember: not always by geography)
2. Identify the key things you need to learn.
3. Identify the <u>initial</u> time-frame for this work.
4. List the people you think that could help you.
5. Identify how you will track your findings.
6. Identify how you will start (Reminder: Begin with what you know and is easy to answer).

Demographics -What do you know about the community / Who are they	Key Dates -Local Holidays -Festivals -Human rights related dates	Local issues -What are the most important local issues? -What do locals care about?
Organisations & Groups	Activist groups / Right Holders / Charities / Social groups / Youth groups / Recreation groups / Businesses	
Decision makers & Influencers	Politicians / Local leaders / Local journalists / Local celebrities / Elders	
Institutions	Local language schools	Community Centres

Capacity assessments: Capacity assessments are a more systematic way of assessing community capacity. They typically involve gathering data on a variety of factors, such as the skills and resources of community members, the strength of community bonds, and the ability of the community to work together. This information can be used to develop a comprehensive picture of community capacity and to identify areas where it needs to be strengthened.

Assessing community capacity is an important first step in developing strategies to improve the community. By understanding the strengths and weaknesses of the community, community leaders can develop more effective interventions.

Here are some specific examples of how community capacity can be assessed:

- A community can assess its capacity to address the problem of crime by conducting a survey of community members to identify the most common crimes in the area. The survey can also ask community members about their perceptions of the police and the criminal justice system. This information can be used to develop strategies to improve public safety'.
- A community can assess its capacity to address the problem of poverty by conducting a community forum to discuss the challenges facing low-income residents. The forum can also identify the resources that are available to help low-income residents. This information can be used to develop strategies to improve economic opportunities for low-income residents.
- A community can assess its capacity to address the problem of environmental pollution by conducting a community mapping project to identify areas of the community that are most affected by pollution. The mapping project can also identify the organizations that are working to address environmental pollution. This information can be used to develop strategies to reduce pollution and improve the environment.

Assessing community capacity is a complex and time-consuming process. However, it is an essential step in developing strategies to improve the community. By understanding the strengths and weaknesses of the community, community leaders can develop more effective interventions that will make a real difference in the lives of community members.

In their 2005 study, Cheers, Cock, Hylton, Keele et al[37]. offer a nuanced exploration of community capacity assessment, emphasizing the need for a comprehensive, multidimensional approach to understand how communities function and respond to challenges. Their work underscores that assessing community capacity involves evaluating various interconnected elements, which collectively determine the community's ability to mobilize resources, engage its members, and tackle local issues.

Cheers et al. (2005) conceptualize community capacity as the collective ability of a community to effectively organize, utilize resources, and engage in collective actions to achieve shared goals. They argue that assessing this capacity requires a detailed examination of several key components.

Social Networks and Relationships are central to understanding community capacity. Cheers et al. highlight the importance of social capital, which encompasses the networks, norms, and social trust that facilitate cooperation and collective action (Putnam, 2000; Coleman, 1988). To evaluate social networks, researchers often use tools such as social network analysis and surveys to gauge the density and quality of relationships within the community. These methods help in understanding how well community members are connected and how these connections support collective efforts.

Leadership and Governance play a critical role in shaping community capacity. Effective leadership, as noted by Cheers et al., is crucial for mobilizing resources, fostering participation, and guiding community initiatives. The assessment of leadership

---

37 Cheers, B. Cock, G. Hilton Keele, L. Kruger & Trigg, H. (2006), 'Measuring community capacity: An electronic auditing tool', in M. Rogers & D. Jones (eds), *The Changing nature of Australia's Country towns*, VURRN Press Ballarat

involves examining both formal leaders, such as elected officials, and informal leaders, who may include respected community members. Techniques for evaluating leadership effectiveness include interviews, surveys, and analyses of leadership styles and impacts (Black & Hughes, 2001).

Resource Availability and Utilization are also essential factors in assessing community capacity. Cheers et al. stress the importance of identifying and evaluating the various resources available within a community, including financial, human, and physical assets. This assessment can be carried out through resource inventories and asset mapping, which help in understanding how these resources are utilized to support community projects and initiatives (Flora, 1998).

Collective Action and Engagement reflect the community's ability to mobilize around common goals. According to Cheers et al., assessing this aspect involves examining the extent and effectiveness of community involvement in decision-making and collective activities. Surveys and focus groups are common methods used to measure participation levels, community engagement in problem-solving, and the impact of collective actions (Sampson et al., 1997).

Shared Values and Norms are integral to fostering community cohesion and action. Cheers et al. discuss how understanding a community's shared values and norms involves exploring the common beliefs and practices among members. Qualitative research methods, such as ethnographic studies and interviews, are valuable for capturing these cultural dimensions and assessing their influence on community capacity (Bourdieu, 1985[38]).

In summary, Cheers, Cock, Hylton, Keele et al. (2005) provide

---

38 Ibid 18

a comprehensive framework for assessing community capacity that includes social networks, leadership, resource availability, collective action, and shared values. This multidimensional approach offers a robust understanding of a community's strengths and challenges, guiding effective strategies for enhancing community development and resilience.

2.5. Summary

"Community Capacity," provides a thorough exploration of the concept and its practical implications. The chapter begins by clarifying foundational concepts crucial to understanding community capacity, including community strength, entrepreneurial social infrastructure, and social capital. It emphasizes the importance of these concepts in fostering individual and collective well-being, social and economic development, and problem-solving within communities.

The chapter highlights the role of community capacity in enabling effective problem resolution and resource mobilization. It discusses various theoretical frameworks, such as the evaluation of community factors by Wilkinson (1970), which explores how social cohesion and resource availability impact community development. This is complemented by insights from Black and Hughes (2001), who define community strength as the resilience and resourcefulness within communities, and by Flora's (1998) concept of entrepreneurial social infrastructure, which examines how local networks drive economic growth.

Additionally, the chapter engages with the notion of social capital, as analyzed by Bordieu (1985), Coleman (1988), Portes (1998), and Putnam (1995). Social capital pertains to the networks, norms, and trust that facilitate community cooperation and enhance collective capabilities. By integrating these frameworks, the chapter offers a comprehensive perspective on assessing and strengthening community capacity, providing valuable insights for practitioners, policymakers, and researchers focused on community development. The discussion underscores the importance of both generic and purpose-specific capacities, the evaluation of social networks and resources, and the role of leadership and shared values in fostering robust and resilient communities.

Useful Websites

Here are some resources and links specific to Australia for assessing community capacity:

1. Australian Government Department of Health

Resource: Community Capacity Building Framework

Description: Provides frameworks and tools for assessing and building community capacity in Australia, focusing on health and social services.

Link: Department of Health Community Capacity Building[39]

2. Australian Institute of Family Studies (AIFS)

Resource: Community Capacity Building and Evaluation Tools

Description: Provides tools and checklists for assessing community capacity, with a focus on family and community support services.

---

39 https://www.dss.gov.au/our-responsibilities/families-and-children/publications-articles/older-evaluation-products/good-practices-and-pitfalls-in-community-based-capacity-building-and-early-intervention-projects-a-toolkit?HTM

Link: AIFS Community Capacity Building[40]

These resources are tailored to the Australian context and provide various tools and frameworks for assessing and enhancing community capacity.

---

40 https://aifs.gov.au/resources/practice-guides/applying-community-capacity-building-approaches-child-welfare-practice

CHAPTER 3

CALD (CULTURALLY AND LINGUISTICALLY DIVERSE) PERSPECTIVE

3.1. Introduction

This chapter aims to:
- Analyze the community groups, faith groups, recreational clubs and different cultural organisations.
- Identify and define community capacity with special insights to CaLD communities; and
- Academic perspective enabling practitioners and communities to asses community capacity

"Bridging Worlds: The 6,000-Year-Old Aboriginal Community Wisdom and the Challenge of Cross-Cultural Understanding"

The Songlines of Australian Aboriginal Culture: Landscape, Loss, and Legacy

The songlines of Australian Aboriginal culture are a profound testament to how Indigenous Australians have understood and navigated the diverse landscapes of their ancient homeland. These intricate systems of oral maps are deeply woven into the cultural and spiritual fabric of Aboriginal life. Unlike conventional maps, songlines encompass not only geographical features but also the rich tapestry of ancestral stories, spiritual beliefs, and ceremonial practices. They are a living, dynamic record of the land, encoded in a form that integrates physical geography with mythological and cultural narratives.

Songlines serve as pathways across the Australian continent, tracing the journeys of ancestral beings who are said to have shaped the land during the Dreamtime, a foundational era in Aboriginal spirituality. Each songline details a specific route through the landscape, describing the interactions between these beings and the natural features they created. As such, songlines are not merely navigational tools but also repositories of cultural knowledge, linking specific places with their mythological significance and guiding the spiritual and practical aspects of daily life.

The oral nature of songlines reflects a broader Aboriginal cultural reliance on spoken rather than written traditions. This system of knowledge transmission has sustained Aboriginal cultures for millennia, allowing them to maintain a deep and holistic understanding of their environment. However, the advent of European colonization brought profound disruptions to this system, particularly through the policies that led to the Stolen Generations. These policies, which forcibly removed Aboriginal children from their families and communities, had devastating effects on the continuity of Aboriginal cultural practices, including the transmission of songlines.

The impact of the Stolen Generations on Aboriginal culture cannot be overstated. The removal of children not only severed familial and communal bonds but also interrupted the transmission of traditional knowledge. The absence of a written language within Aboriginal cultures meant that this knowledge was entirely dependent on oral traditions. With the forced displacement and cultural dislocation caused by the Stolen Generations, many children grew up without the opportunity to learn and practice their cultural heritage, including the essential songlines that connect them to their ancestral past.

This loss has had a profound effect on Aboriginal identity and the cohesion of Indigenous communities. For many Aboriginal people, the disconnection from songlines and other traditional practices represents a deeper loss of cultural continuity and identity. The younger generations, who have often grown up with fragmented or incomplete cultural knowledge, face challenges in reconnecting with their ancestral heritage. The disruption of oral traditions has contributed to a sense of cultural dislocation and a diminished capacity to sustain traditional practices, which are vital for maintaining community cohesion and cultural identity.

The importance of written language in this context is significant. While Aboriginal cultures traditionally relied on oral methods for knowledge transmission, the introduction of written forms of communication could help preserve and document cultural practices that are at risk of being lost. Written records could serve as a complementary tool to oral traditions, offering a means to safeguard and transmit cultural knowledge more effectively across generations. The integration of written documentation alongside oral practices could provide a means to stabilize and reinforce cultural continuity, ensuring that traditional knowledge is not lost to future generations.

The importance of passing on traditional knowledge and practices cannot be understated. For Aboriginal communities, songlines are not just historical records but living traditions that guide spiritual practices, social organization, and environmental management. The disruption of this transmission has had lasting consequences for Aboriginal identity and community resilience. Restoring and revitalizing traditional knowledge involves not only recovering lost practices but also addressing the broader impacts of colonization, including the need for healing and reconciliation.

Efforts to bridge the gap between traditional Aboriginal knowledge and contemporary practices must be approached with sensitivity and respect. This involves acknowledging the historical injustices faced by Aboriginal peoples and working collaboratively to support the revitalization of cultural practices. By valuing both oral traditions and written documentation, there is potential to foster a more inclusive approach to cultural preservation. This integration can enhance the capacity of Aboriginal communities to sustain their cultural heritage and strengthen their sense of identity.

The importance of the written documents and emancipation of knowledge towards the younger CaLD generations.

The 'songlines' of Australian Aboriginal culture represent a complex and deeply meaningful way of understanding the landscape, intertwining geography with spirituality and cultural knowledge. The impact of the Stolen Generations has highlighted the crucial need to address the gaps created by the loss of oral traditions and the absence of written language. By recognizing the importance of passing on traditional knowledge and considering the role of written documentation in preserving cultural practices, we can work towards a more inclusive and respectful approach to cultural heritage. This effort is essential for supporting the resilience and identity of Aboriginal communities and ensuring that their rich cultural legacy endures for future generations.

Australia's demographic landscape is profoundly shaped by its history of migration and the presence of culturally and linguistically diverse (CALD) communities. The nation's migration patterns have evolved significantly, particularly since the mid-20th century, reflecting broader global trends and changes in immigration policies. Initially, Australia's immigration policy was primarily focused on attracting European migrants post-World War II. However, since the 1970s, the country has embraced a more inclusive approach, welcoming individuals from a variety of regions including Asia, the Middle East, and Africa (Jupp, 2002[41]; Markus, 2010[42]).

As of the 2021 Census, nearly half of Australia's population was born overseas or had at least one parent born overseas, highlighting the country's extensive multicultural makeup (Australian Bureau of Statistics, 2021[43]). The census data also reveals that over 300 languages are spoken in Australian households, with Mandarin, Arabic, and Italian being among the most prevalent (Australian Bureau of Statistics, 2022). This linguistic diversity underscores the rich cultural tapestry that CALD communities contribute to Australian society.

---

41 Jupp, J. (2002) From White Australia to Woomera: The Story of Australian Immigration. West Nyack, NY: Cambridge University Press

42 Markus, A. & Arnup, J. (2010). Mapping Social Cohesion 2009: The Scanlon Foundations Surveys Full Report (2010), section 12

43 ABS (2021)

However, migrant and CALD communities encounter a range of challenges. Language barriers are a significant issue, impacting access to services, employment opportunities, and social integration. To address these challenges, the Australian government has implemented programs like the Adult Migrant English Program (AMEP), which provides English language training to newly arrived migrants (Department of Home Affairs, 2021). Despite these efforts, issues persist, including difficulties in accessing essential services due to language and cultural differences, and discrimination in the labor market that affects employment outcomes and economic stability (Cooper, 2020[44]; Hugo, 2011[45]).

Cultural adjustment presents another layer of complexity. Migrants often face challenges in adapting to new social norms and practices, which can affect their overall well-being and integration into Australian society (Hollinsworth, 2006[46]). These challenges are compounded by systemic issues such as limited access to culturally appropriate services, which can impact areas like health, education, and social welfare (McKinnon, 2013[47]).

Despite these hurdles, CALD communities make invaluable contributions to Australian society. They enrich the cultural

---

44 Cooper, R & Foley, M. (2020), *Workplace gender equality in the post-pandemic era: Where to next,* Journal of Industrial Relations 2021, Vol. 63(4)

45 Hugo, G (2014) 'The Economic Contribution of Humanitarian Settlers in Australia', International Migration, vol.52, no.2, pp. 32-52.

46 Hollinsworth, D. (2006). Confronting racism in communities: Guidelines and resources for anti-racism training workshops. Centre for Multicultural Pastoral Care, Paddington, QLD and the University of the Sunshine Coast, Queensland.

47 McKinnon, J. (2013). The Environment: A Private Concern or a Professional Practice Issue for Australian Social Workers? *Australian Social Work,* 66(2), 156–170. https://doi.org/10.1080/0312407X.2013.782558

landscape through diverse traditions, cuisines, and festivals. Economically, migrants contribute significantly by filling skill shortages and driving entrepreneurship (Birrell et al., 2019[48]). Recognizing these contributions is crucial for fostering a more inclusive society.

To support CALD communities effectively, ongoing policy efforts are necessary. The Australian government's Multicultural Policy aims to promote social cohesion and support cultural diversity (Australian Government, 2021). Additionally, organizations like the Federation of Ethnic Communities' Councils of Australia (FECCA) play a pivotal role in advocating for the needs and interests of ethnic communities (FECCA, 2022). Moving forward, addressing the needs of CALD communities requires a continued focus on improving language services, combating discrimination, and enhancing cultural competence across public services (Pillai, 2022[49]).

3.2. CaLD Cultural Perspective

The discourse surrounding migrant challenges in Australia is deeply intertwined with broader societal dynamics, including high-profile events such as the Cronulla riots. These riots, which erupted in December 2005, serve as a stark reminder of the tensions that can arise between different cultural groups and highlight the complex interplay of migration, identity, and social cohesion.

The Cronulla riots began as a local confrontation in the beachside

---

48 Birrell, B., & McCloskey, D. (2019). Australia's' jobs and growth'strategy: pathway to a low productivity economy.

49 Pillai, J. (2022). Cultural Mapping: A Guide to Understanding Place, Community and Continuity (: Revised and Updated). Strategic Information and Research Development Centre.

suburb of Cronulla, Sydney, but quickly escalated into a wider conflict characterized by racial and cultural overtones. Initially sparked by a violent altercation involving local residents and individuals of Lebanese descent, the riots grew into a more extensive and violent outburst of racial hostility, predominantly directed towards people of Middle Eastern appearance (Morris, 2006[50]). The events at Cronulla exposed underlying issues related to migration and integration, drawing attention to the challenges faced by migrant communities in Australia.

Migrants in Australia often confront a myriad of difficulties that can affect their integration and well-being. Language barriers are one of the most significant challenges. Despite government initiatives like the Adult Migrant English Program (AMEP), which provides English language training to new arrivals, many migrants still struggle with limited proficiency. This language gap can impede their ability to access essential services, secure employment, and fully participate in social and civic life (Department of Home Affairs, 2021). Language is more than a communication tool; it is a bridge to economic opportunities, social inclusion, and cultural integration.

Employment discrimination adds another layer of complexity to the migrant experience. Research has shown that many migrants face biases in the labor market, which can limit their employment prospects and economic advancement (Cooper, 2020). The recognition of overseas qualifications is another critical issue; migrants often find that their professional credentials are not fully acknowledged in Australia, which can prevent them from securing jobs that

---

50 Morris, E. W. (2006). An unexpected minority: White kids in an urban school. Rutgers University Press.

match their skills and experience (Hugo, 2011[51]). This not only affects their economic stability but also their sense of inclusion and professional identity.

Cultural adjustment is a further challenge that migrants face. Adapting to new social norms and practices in Australia can be a daunting process, particularly for those who have recently arrived. This adjustment is often accompanied by the stress of navigating unfamiliar systems and dealing with the pressure to balance maintaining one's cultural heritage while integrating into Australian society (Hollinsworth, 2006[52]). The systemic issues that migrants face, including the lack of culturally sensitive services, can exacerbate these difficulties and hinder their overall adjustment (Swan & McKinnon, 2008[53]).

The Cronulla riots brought these issues to the forefront, illustrating the tensions that can arise when cultural and social divides are not adequately addressed. The aftermath of the riots highlighted the urgent need for dialogue and understanding between different community groups. It underscored the importance of addressing underlying social issues, such as racism and discrimination, which can fuel conflict and hinder social cohesion.

In the wake of the Cronulla riots, there has been a concerted

---

[51] Hugo, G 2011, 'A significant contribution: The economic, social and civic contributions of first and second generation humanitarian entrant's summary of findings Australian Government: Department of Social Services', https://www.dss.gov.au/

[52] Hollinsworth, D. (2006). Race and Racism in Australia. (3rd ed.) Thomson Learning Australia.

[53] McKinnon, S. L. (2008). Unsettling resettlement: Problematizing "Lost Boys of Sudan" resettlement and identity. Western Journal of Communication, 72(4), 397-414.

effort to promote intercultural dialogue and foster greater understanding among Australia's diverse communities. Initiatives aimed at improving social cohesion and addressing the challenges faced by migrants have become more prominent. The Australian government's Multicultural Policy, for example, seeks to support cultural diversity and promote inclusivity, while organizations like the Federation of Ethnic Communities' Councils of Australia (FECCA) work to advocate for the needs of ethnic communities and address issues of discrimination and exclusion (Australian Government, 2021; FECCA, 2022).

In conclusion, the challenges faced by migrant communities in Australia are complex and multifaceted, encompassing language barriers, employment discrimination, and cultural adjustment. The Cronulla riots serve as a stark reminder of the need for ongoing efforts to address these challenges and foster social cohesion. By promoting understanding and inclusivity, Australia can work towards a more integrated and harmonious society where the contributions of its diverse migrant communities are fully recognized and valued.

3.3. Working with CaLD communities

Legal perspective in working with migrant communities
Working with migrant communities from a legal perspective requires a nuanced understanding of the various legal frameworks and protections that safeguard their rights and ensure equitable treatment. The primary legal instruments guiding interactions with migrants in Australia include the *Migration Act 1958*[54], which regu-

---

54 *Migration Act 1958* (Cth).

lates the entry, stay, and removal of non-citizens, and the *Australian Human Rights Commission Act 1986*[55], which oversees the enforcement of human rights protections, including those related to race, nationality, and ethnicity.

The *Migration Act* outlines the criteria for visa applications, the rights of visa holders, and the conditions under which visas can be revoked or cancelled. It establishes a legal basis for managing migration, but it also implies significant responsibilities for ensuring that migrants are treated fairly and according to their legal entitlements (Department of Home Affairs, 2022). Alongside this, the *Racial Discrimination Act 1975* provides crucial protections against racial discrimination in various contexts, including employment, education, and access to services. This legislation ensures that individuals are not discriminated against based on their race, color, descent, or national or ethnic origin (Australian Human Rights Commission, 2022). This legal protection is essential for maintaining an inclusive environment for migrant communities.

Employment law also plays a significant role in the protection of migrant workers. The *Fair Work Act 2009* stipulates the rights of all employees, including migrants, to fair wages, safe working conditions, and protection against unfair dismissal (Fair Work Ombudsman, 2023). Employers are legally obligated to comply with these standards, which include addressing issues such as exploitation and ensuring that migrant workers receive fair treatment. Migrant workers must be protected against unfair practices that could arise due to language barriers, cultural differences, or other factors.

Legal professionals and service providers must be adept at

---

55 *Australian Human Rights Commission Act 1986*

navigating these legal frameworks while being sensitive to the unique needs of migrant communities. This involves offering services in a culturally competent manner and ensuring that all legal processes are accessible and understandable. For instance, providing legal assistance in multiple languages or using interpreters can help bridge communication gaps and ensure that migrants fully understand their rights and obligations (Legal Aid Commission, 2022).

Access to justice is another critical concern. Migrant communities may face barriers to legal aid and support due to financial constraints or limited knowledge of their rights. Legal aid organizations play a vital role in offering free or low-cost legal services, which are crucial for addressing a wide range of issues, from immigration status to employment disputes and family law matters (Legal Aid Commission, 2022).

In conclusion, working with migrant communities from a legal perspective involves a comprehensive understanding of migration laws, anti-discrimination regulations, and employment protections. It requires a commitment to ensuring that all interactions and services are legally compliant while being culturally sensitive and accessible. By integrating legal expertise with an understanding of the diverse needs of migrant communities, professionals can better support these individuals in navigating their legal challenges and achieving fair and just outcomes.

Enhancing Lives: The Rewards of Working with Migrants
Working with migrant communities can be a rewarding experience, but it can also be challenging. Here are some tips on how to work effectively with migrant communities:

i. Start by building relationships. Migrant communities are

diverse, and each community has its own unique needs and challenges. It's important to take the time to get to know the members of the community and to build relationships with them. This will help you to understand their needs and to develop programs and services that are tailored to their specific needs.

ii. Be culturally sensitive. Each migrant community has its own culture and traditions. It's important to be respectful of these cultures and traditions, and to avoid making assumptions about the community.

iii. Use interpreters. If you don't speak the language of the migrant community, it's important to use interpreters. This will help you to communicate effectively with the community and to ensure that they understand the services that you are providing.

iv. Be patient. Migrant communities may have experienced trauma or discrimination, and they may be hesitant to trust outsiders. It's important to be patient with the community, and to give them time to build trust with you.

v. Be flexible. Migrant communities are constantly changing, and their needs may change over time. It's important to be flexible and to be willing to adapt your programs and services to meet the changing needs of the community.

vi. Partner with community organizations. There are often community organizations that are already working with migrant communities. Partnering with these organizations can help you to reach a wider audience and to provide more comprehensive services.

vii. Get involved in the community. One of the best ways to build relationships with migrant communities is to get involved in the community. This could involve attending community events, volunteering with community organizations, or simply getting to know your neighbours.

By following these tips, you can build strong relationships with migrant communities and help them to thrive.

3.4. Summary

This chapter delves into the multifaceted landscape of Australia's culturally and linguistically diverse (CALD) communities, examining their challenges, opportunities, and the capacity for community engagement. Australia's demographic shifts since the mid-20th century reflect significant changes in migration patterns. Initially focused on European migration, Australian immigration policies have evolved to embrace a broader range of origins, including Asia, the Middle East, and Africa (Jupp, 2007[56]; Markus, 2019). The 2021 Census reveals that nearly half of Australia's population is either born overseas or has at least one foreign-born parent, with over 300 languages spoken across households (Australian Bureau of Statistics, 2021, 2022). This linguistic diversity underscores the rich cultural contributions of CALD communities.

However, these communities face considerable challenges. Language barriers remain a major obstacle, affecting access to services and employment. The Adult Migrant English Program (AMEP) aims to address these issues by providing English language training, yet many migrants continue to struggle with limited proficiency, impacting their integration and opportunities (Department of Home Affairs, 2021). Employment discrimination further

---

56 Ibid 41

compounds these difficulties, with many migrants facing biases and challenges in having their qualifications recognized, which affects their professional prospects and economic stability (Cooper, 2020; Hugo, 2011[57]).

Cultural adjustment is another significant challenge, as migrants navigate new social norms while maintaining their cultural identity. The Cronulla riots of 2005, which highlighted racial tensions and the complexities of cultural integration, emphasize the need for ongoing dialogue and understanding among community groups (Morris, 2006). The aftermath of these riots has prompted increased efforts to foster intercultural understanding and support through policies like the Australian Multicultural Policy and advocacy by organizations such as the Federation of Ethnic Communities' Councils of Australia (FECCA) (Australian Government, 2021; FECCA, 2022).

Effective engagement with CALD communities requires a culturally sensitive approach, building relationships, using interpreters, and adapting to their evolving needs. Partnerships with community organizations and active involvement in local events are crucial for understanding and addressing the unique challenges faced by these communities. By promoting inclusivity and addressing systemic issues, Australia can enhance social cohesion and fully leverage the contributions of its diverse migrant populations.

---

57 Ibid 45

Useful Websites
1. Multicultural Australia
Provides information and resources to support multiculturalism and diversity in Australia. - https://www.multiculturalaustralia.org.au/
2. Settlement Services International (SSI)
Offers support services for refugees and migrants, including assistance with settlement and community integration. - https://www.ssi.org.au/
3. The Federation of Ethnic Communities' Councils of Australia (FECCA)
Advocates for the needs of CALD communities and provides resources and information on policy and services. - https://fecca.org.au/
4. Ethnic Communities' Council of Victoria (ECCV)
Focuses on promoting the interests and needs of Victoria's CALD communities through advocacy and support. - https://eccv.org.au/
5. Australian Human Rights Commission (AHRC)
Provides information on human rights issues, including those affecting CALD communities, and offers resources for support. - https://humanrights.gov.au/
6. NSW Service for the Treatment and Rehabilitation of Torture and Trauma Survivors (STARTTS)
Offers support and services for individuals and communities affected by torture and trauma, with a focus on CALD groups. -https://humanrights.gov.au/

These websites offer a range of resources, support services, and advocacy for individuals and communities from diverse cultural and linguistic backgrounds.

PART TWO

WORKING WITH COMMUNITIES

In Part 2 of this book, titled "Working with Communities," we delve into the nuanced methods and theoretical frameworks essential for effective community engagement and development.

Chapter 4 provides a thorough evaluation of conceptual approaches in capacity building. The discussion centers on the importance of fostering capacity before service delivery, emphasizing how foundational support and preparation can significantly enhance the effectiveness of subsequent initiatives. The chapter further explores developmental approaches that prioritize people over programs, advocating for strategies that focus on empowering individuals and communities as a whole rather than merely implementing predetermined solutions.

Chapter 5 builds on these ideas by developing a typology of approaches to community work. It introduces the concept of participative democracy as a broader framework to enhance both 'community empowerment' and 'developmental' approaches. This chapter outlines how participative democracy can facilitate more inclusive decision-making processes and strengthen community involvement in shaping their own futures.

Chapter 6 shifts the focus to government approaches to working with communities. It examines the various strategies employed by government bodies to engage with and support communities but refrains from evaluating the outcomes of these approaches directly. Instead, it highlights the importance of developing a comprehensive measurement matrix that incorporates diverse evaluative frameworks. This matrix aims to address the challenge of capturing the varied aspirations and outcomes of different communities, recognizing that such a task is inherently complex due to the unique goals and needs of each community.

Together, these chapters offer a rich exploration of how conceptual and practical approaches can be applied to effectively work with and empower communities, while also acknowledging the challenges and complexities involved in measuring success and impact.

CHAPTER 4

COMMUNITY - CONCEPTS AND LITERATURE

4.1. Introduction

This chapter will:
- Define the four conceptual approaches: We begin by examining four distinct conceptual approaches that provide a framework for community work. Each approach offers unique insights and methodologies for enhancing community engagement and building capacity. By dissecting these approaches, we aim to highlight their respective strengths and applications in real-world contexts.
- Explain the terms: A clear understanding of key terms is crucial for navigating the complexities of community work. This section defines the essential concepts and terminology used throughout the chapter, ensuring a common language and framework for discussing community development strategies.
- Importance in relationships: **The Threads That Weave Through Communities** - Central to any discussion of community is the

intricate web of relationships that binds individuals together. This section explores how these connections form the fabric of community life, influencing both the challenges and opportunities faced by communities. We delve into how understanding and fostering these relationships can enhance the effectiveness of community interventions.

- Significance of reflections and assess the practical worksheets: To bridge theory and practice, this chapter includes reflections and practical worksheets designed to help you apply the conceptual approaches to real-life scenarios. These tools are intended to encourage critical thinking and provide hands-on experience in implementing the strategies discussed.
- Organizations, governments and funding agencies to create sustainable organic growth in communities.
- Summary: Finally, we summarize the key points covered in the chapter, consolidating the insights gained from the conceptual approaches, definitions, and practical applications. This summary serves as a recap of the essential elements needed for effective community work and provides a foundation for further exploration in subsequent chapters.
- Through this comprehensive overview, the chapter aims to equip you with a robust understanding of community dynamics and the tools necessary for fostering positive and impactful development.

4.2. Four conceptual approaches

In the field of community development, several conceptual approaches provide valuable frameworks for understanding and implementing effective strategies. Research by Zakus and Lysack[58], Oakley and Marsden[59], Dwyer[60], and Midgley[61] offers significant insights into these approaches, which include the contributions approach, the instrumental approach, the community empowerment approach, and the development approach.

The Contributions Approach emphasizes the importance of recognizing and valuing the contributions that community members make to their own development. Zakus and Lysack (1998)[62] argue that this approach focuses on understanding how individuals and groups within a community contribute their time, skills, and resources toward collective goals. By acknowledging these contributions, community development efforts can build on existing local assets and foster a greater sense of ownership and participation among community members. Their research highlights that valuing these contributions not only enhances the effectiveness of development initiatives but also strengthens community cohesion and resilience.

The Instrumental Approach is characterized by its focus on achieving specific, often measurable, outcomes through targeted

---

58 Zakus, J.D., Lysack, C.L. (1998). Revisiting community participation. Journal of health policy and planning, 13(1), 1-12

59 Oakley, P. and Marsden, D. (1982) "Radical community development in the Third World", in Craig, G., Derricourt, N., and Loney, M. (eds.). Community Work and the State, L

60 Dwyer, C. (1999). Contradictions of community: questions of identity for young British Muslim women. Environment and Planning A, 31(1), 53-68.

61 Midgley, G., & Ochoa-Arias, A. (Eds.). (2004). Community operational research: OR and systems thinking for community development. Springer Science & Business Media.

62 Ibid 58

interventions. Oakley and Marsden (1984)[63] describe this approach as one that prioritizes the use of resources and strategies to accomplish particular objectives, such as improving infrastructure or delivering services. This approach is pragmatic, seeking to use interventions as tools to address defined needs and achieve tangible results. Research indicates that while the instrumental approach can lead to clear and immediate benefits, it may sometimes overlook broader contextual factors and the long-term sustainability of development efforts.

The Community Empowerment Approach centers on enhancing the capacity of community members to take control over their own lives and development. Dwyer (1998)[64] and Midgley (1995)[65] emphasize that empowerment involves enabling individuals and groups to participate actively in decision-making processes and to influence the outcomes that affect them. This approach aims to build the skills, confidence, and resources necessary for communities to advocate for their needs and drive their own development. Research supports that empowering communities leads to more sustainable and equitable outcomes, as it fosters greater engagement and ownership of development initiatives. Empowered communities are better equipped to address their challenges and leverage opportunities for growth.

The Development Approach, as discussed by Zakus and Lysack (1998) and Midgley (1995), encompasses a broader perspective on community growth and transformation. This approach focuses on the overall improvement of social, economic, and environmental

---

63 Ibid 59

64 Ibid 60

65 Ibid 61

conditions within a community. It incorporates elements from the contributions and empowerment approaches but places a stronger emphasis on long-term, systemic change. Development approaches aim to create comprehensive strategies that address the root causes of issues and promote sustainable progress. Research indicates that successful development approaches require careful planning, stakeholder collaboration, and a focus on both immediate and future needs.

Together, these approaches offer a multifaceted understanding of community development. The contributions approach highlights the importance of leveraging local resources, the instrumental approach focuses on achieving specific outcomes, the community empowerment approach emphasizes local control and participation, and the development approach seeks holistic and sustainable improvements. Integrating these perspectives allows for a more nuanced and effective approach to community development, addressing both immediate needs and long-term goals.

4.3. Defining Terms

In the field of community development, precise definitions of key terms are crucial for fostering a shared understanding and effective practice. This section aims to clarify fundamental concepts commonly encountered in community development discourse, facilitating a more nuanced and actionable engagement with the subject.

Community Development refers to a process through which community members come together to identify and address collective needs, build upon their strengths, and enhance their overall well-being. It encompasses a range of activities aimed at improving social, economic, and environmental conditions through collaborative efforts and local initiatives. The process is inherently participatory, involving various stakeholders in identifying priorities, planning interventions, and implementing strategies for sustainable change.

Capacity Building is a core concept in community development, focusing on strengthening the skills, knowledge, and resources of individuals and organizations within a community. The aim is to empower local entities to effectively address their own needs and challenges. Capacity building involves training, education, and the provision of resources that enhance the ability of community members to engage in development activities and make informed decisions.

Empowerment in community development refers to the process of enabling individuals and groups to gain control over their own lives and actively participate in decision-making processes that affect them. Empowerment emphasizes the importance of increasing local agency and self-efficacy, allowing communities to influence outcomes and drive their own development. It often involves addressing power imbalances and fostering an environment where marginalized voices can be heard and valued.

Participatory Approaches are methods used to involve community members actively in the planning, implementation, and evaluation of development projects. These approaches are grounded in the belief that those directly affected by development initiatives should have a central role in shaping them. Participatory approaches can enhance the relevance and effectiveness of interventions by ensuring they are aligned with the actual needs and priorities of the community.

Social Capital refers to the networks, relationships, and norms of trust and reciprocity that facilitate cooperation and collective action within a community. Social capital is considered a vital resource for community development, as it influences the ability of community members to work together towards common goals. High levels of social capital can lead to improved social cohesion, better health outcomes, and more effective problem-solving.

Asset-Based Community Development (ABCD) is a framework that focuses on identifying and mobilizing the existing strengths and resources within a community rather than focusing on its needs or deficiencies. This approach builds on the idea that communities are rich with assets—such as skills, knowledge, and local networks—that can be harnessed to drive positive change and development. By leveraging these assets, ABCD seeks to create sustainable and community-driven outcomes.

Sustainability in the context of community development refers to the ability of development initiatives to continue to deliver benefits over the long term. Sustainable development aims to ensure that the improvements achieved through community efforts are maintained and that future generations can also benefit from the outcomes. This involves considering environmental, economic, and social factors to create resilient and adaptive communities.

Inclusivity is a principle that ensures that all community members, particularly those from marginalized or disadvantaged groups, have the opportunity to participate in and benefit from development activities. Inclusivity addresses issues of equity and justice, striving to create processes and outcomes that reflect the diverse needs and perspectives of the entire community.

By defining these terms, we establish a common language that

Figure 5: Individual within the larger community

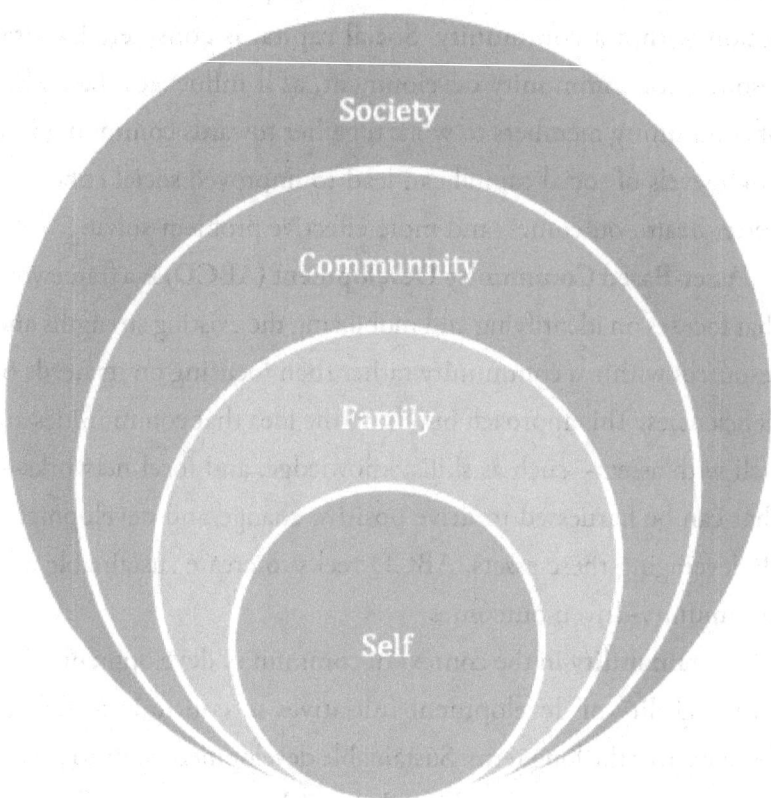

enhances clarity and coherence in community development practice. Understanding and applying these concepts effectively is essential for designing and implementing strategies that are both responsive to local needs and conducive to long-term, sustainable growth.

In community development, understanding the nuanced definitions and interconnections of self, family, community, and society is crucial for designing effective and comprehensive interventions. These concepts are deeply interrelated and influence one another in significant ways. Drawing on the work of Brown (2002[66]), Himmelman (1996)[67], Mohr (1988[68]), and Spekman (2000[69]), we can elucidate these definitions and their interconnections in greater detail.

Self - refers to an individual's sense of identity, personal agency, and self-concept. Brown (1999) argues that the self is not a fixed entity but rather a dynamic construct shaped by personal experiences and social interactions. The self encompasses one's self-perception, aspirations, and the roles one assumes within various social contexts. In community development, a well-developed sense of self is essential for individuals to engage effectively with community initiatives and contribute to collective efforts. An individual's self-efficacy and personal empowerment are critical for meaningful participation in community development, as they determine how one interacts with and influences broader social structures.

Family is defined as the primary social unit consisting of individuals related by blood, marriage, or chosen relationships. According to Himmelman (1996), families play a foundational role in socialization, providing emotional support, resources, and values that shape individual behavior and capacity. In the context of community development, families are crucial for nurturing personal growth

---

[66] Brown, D. L. (2002). Migration and Community: Social Networks in a Multilevel World. Rural Sociology, 67(1).

[67] Himmelman, A. T. (1996). PART TWO. Creating Collaborative Advantage, 19.

[68] Mohr, J. W. (1998). Measuring meaning structures. Annual review of sociology, 24(1), 345-370.

[69] Speckman, M. (2014). Towards an asset-based model: A critical reflection on student material support with special reference to clienthood/citizenship tension. Perspectives on student affairs in South Africa, 121.

and supporting community involvement. The stability and dynamics within families—such as support structures, communication patterns, and resource availability—impact both individual development and community cohesion. Strong family units contribute to the health of communities by fostering responsible, engaged citizens and supporting local development efforts.

Community is understood as a collective of individuals who interact within a shared geographical area or around common interests, creating a network of relationships and social institutions. Mohr (1988[70]) describes the community as a complex system where local organizations, institutions, and social networks work together to address common needs and facilitate collective action. Community development focuses on harnessing local assets, building social capital, and fostering active engagement among community members. The effectiveness of development initiatives often depends on the strength of these networks and the ability to mobilize community resources. The health of a community is influenced by individual contributions, family dynamics, and the support of broader societal structures.

Society encompasses the larger social, economic, and political systems within which communities exist. Spekman (2000[71]) highlights that society includes various institutions and norms that regulate individual and collective behavior on a broader scale. Societal frameworks provide the context for community functioning, influencing resource allocation, policy, and overall development opportunities. The impact of societal conditions on community development is profound, as broader economic trends, legislation,

---

70 Ibid 68

71 Ibid 69

and cultural norms shape the environment in which communities operate. Conversely, the collective actions and well-being of communities can influence societal norms and policies, creating a dynamic interplay between local and broader social systems.

The interconnections between self, family, community, and society are intricate and reciprocal. The self is shaped by family experiences and community interactions, while it also contributes to both. Family structures influence the development of the self and affect community dynamics by providing the foundational support that enables individuals to engage with their communities. Communities, in turn, function within the broader societal context, which sets the parameters for their development and functioning. The societal framework impacts community development through policies, economic conditions, and cultural norms, while communities can influence societal change through collective action and advocacy.

These interconnections underscore the need for a multi-dimensional approach to community development, recognizing that addressing issues at the level of individual self-concept, family dynamics, community engagement, and societal structures is essential for creating sustainable and inclusive development strategies. By understanding and leveraging these relationships, practitioners can design more effective interventions that address the complexities of human and social systems.

4.4. Relationships – The threads that weave through communities
In the realm of community development, the establishment of partnerships and relationships is fundamental to fostering sustainable

and impactful initiatives. Dowling et al. (2004[72]) provide a comprehensive framework for understanding the critical role that these connections play in weaving the fabric of thriving communities.

Dowling et al. (2004[73]) argue that partnerships and relationships are not merely adjuncts to community development efforts but are integral to their success. These connections act as the threads that weave together various community elements, creating a cohesive and resilient social fabric. The ability to forge effective partnerships and build robust relationships directly influences the effectiveness of community interventions and the achievement of development goals.

Partnerships in community development involve collaboration between diverse stakeholders, including local organizations, government entities, businesses, and community members. Dowling et al. (2004) emphasize that successful partnerships are characterized by mutual respect, shared goals, and clear communication. Establishing these partnerships requires a deep understanding of the stakeholders' needs, capabilities, and resources. Effective partnerships leverage the strengths of each participant, creating synergies that enhance the overall capacity to address community issues. They enable the pooling of resources, sharing of expertise, and alignment of efforts towards common objectives, thus maximizing the impact of development initiatives.

Relationships are the interpersonal and organizational connections that underpin successful partnerships. According to Dowling et al. (2004), the quality of these relationships significantly affects

---

[72] Dowling, B., Powell, M., Glendenning, C. (2004) 'Conceptualizing successful partnerships', *Health and Social care in the Community*, Vol. 12, no. 4, pp. 309-17

[73] Ibid

the efficiency and sustainability of community development projects. Building strong, trust-based relationships involves engaging with community members and stakeholders on a personal level, understanding their perspectives, and fostering open dialogue. These relationships help to establish a foundation of trust and collaboration, which is essential for overcoming challenges and achieving shared goals. The strength of these connections often determines the level of community buy-in and the willingness of stakeholders to contribute to and support development efforts.

The Threads that Weave Through Communities metaphorically represent the interconnectedness of various relationships and partnerships within a community. Dowling et al. (2004[74]) highlight that these threads are critical for creating a network of support and cooperation that binds different elements of the community together. This interconnectedness ensures that community development efforts are not isolated or fragmented but are part of a larger, coordinated strategy. By weaving these threads effectively, practitioners can create a more resilient and adaptive community, capable of responding to both opportunities and challenges.

The establishment of partnerships and relationships also involves addressing potential conflicts and power dynamics. Dowling et al. (2004) note that understanding and navigating these dynamics is crucial for maintaining productive collaborations. Successful community development practitioners are adept at managing diverse interests and fostering an environment where all voices are heard and valued. This approach helps to ensure that partnerships remain equitable and that the benefits of development efforts are shared broadly across the community.

---

74 Ibid 72

In conclusion, the insights provided by Dowling et al. (2004) underscore the importance of partnerships and relationships as foundational elements in community development. These connections serve as the threads that weave together the various components of a community, creating a unified and resilient social fabric. By prioritizing the establishment of effective partnerships and nurturing strong relationships, community development practitioners can enhance the impact of their initiatives and foster a more cohesive and sustainable community.

'Elements' of Community development work

In community development, structuring effective initiatives requires a comprehensive approach that addresses both the practical and transformative aspects of community engagement. Susan Kenny's (1999[75]) six elements—Information, Authenticity, Vision, Pragmatism, Strategy, and Transformation—provide a robust framework for structuring community development work, ensuring that efforts are both impactful and sustainable.

Information serves as the foundation of community development efforts. It involves gathering and analyzing data to understand the needs, strengths, and dynamics of the community. Accurate and relevant information helps practitioners identify key issues, set priorities, and tailor interventions to meet the specific needs of the community. By ensuring that decisions are informed by solid data, practitioners can enhance the relevance and effectiveness of their initiatives, fostering greater community trust and engagement.

Authenticity is crucial for building genuine relationships and

---

75 Kenny, S., & Connors, P. (2017). *Developing Communities for the Future* (5th ed.). South Melbourne: Cengage Learning Australia.

credibility within the community. Practitioners must approach their work with sincerity and integrity, demonstrating a genuine commitment to the community's well-being. Authenticity involves listening to community members, valuing their perspectives, and engaging with them in meaningful ways. This element fosters trust and respect, which are essential for successful collaboration and for ensuring that development efforts are aligned with the community's values and needs.

Vision provides direction and inspiration for community development work. It involves articulating a clear and compelling vision for the future of the community, which serves as a guiding light for all development efforts. A well-defined vision helps to unify stakeholders around common goals and motivates collective action. By creating and communicating a shared vision, practitioners can align efforts, inspire commitment, and drive progress towards achieving long-term objectives.

Pragmatism - when applied in community development, involves adopting a practical approach that acknowledges current realities while striving for feasible improvements. This perspective is especially critical when dealing with individuals or groups caught in the 'politics of despair,' where there is a tendency to feel disillusioned with existing structures and to succumb to a passive state of wishing for different circumstances rather than actively working towards change.

The 'politics of despair' is characterized by a sense of frustration and resignation, where individuals feel overwhelmed by systemic inadequacies and may retreat into inaction, believing that meaningful change is unattainable. In such a state, there is often a focus on the perceived deficiencies of current systems rather than on proactive solutions. Pragmatism offers a way to counter this inaction by emphasizing what can realistically be done within the existing constraints.

In this context, pragmatism involves recognizing and accepting the limitations of current systems without allowing these constraints to paralyze action. It requires a shift from idealistic visions of what should be to a more grounded approach of what can be achieved given the current circumstances. This practical mindset focuses on incremental progress rather than waiting for perfect conditions or sweeping systemic changes that might seem out of reach.

Rather than dwelling on the inadequacies of existing structures, a pragmatic approach encourages individuals and communities to identify and act on immediate opportunities for improvement. This involves setting realistic goals and focusing on achievable steps that can make a tangible difference. By addressing smaller, manageable aspects of the broader issue, individuals can start to see progress and regain a sense of agency.

Pragmatism also involves leveraging existing resources and strengths within the community. Instead of waiting for external support or ideal conditions, it emphasizes making the best use of what is already available. This approach helps build confidence and momentum, showing that change is possible even within the constraints of current systems.

Furthermore, a pragmatic approach fosters active participation and engagement. By involving people directly in the process of problem-solving and decision-making, practitioners can help shift individuals from passive dissatisfaction to active involvement. This engagement not only empowers individuals but also aligns their efforts with practical, achievable outcomes, thus fostering a more hopeful and proactive attitude.

Ultimately, pragmatism in this context aims to break the cycle of despair by demonstrating that meaningful progress is possible through realistic and actionable steps. It encourages a shift from merely wishing for change to actively pursuing achievable goals, thereby transforming feelings of helplessness into opportunities for constructive action. By focusing on what can be done now, rather than what is ideal, pragmatism helps communities overcome inertia and work towards sustainable improvement.

Strategy involves the deliberate planning and execution of actions designed to achieve the community's development goals. It encompasses setting objectives, designing interventions, and allocating resources in a way that maximizes impact. A well-crafted strategy outlines the steps necessary to realize the community's vision, providing a roadmap for implementation. Strategic planning ensures that efforts are coherent, coordinated, and aligned with the overall goals of the development initiative.

Transformation reflects the ultimate goal of community development work: fostering meaningful and lasting change within the community. It involves not only addressing current issues but also creating conditions that enable the community to thrive in the long term. Transformation is about empowering community members, building resilience, and fostering a culture of continuous improvement and adaptation. By focusing on transformative outcomes, practitioners aim to create sustainable impacts that enhance the community's capacity to address future challenges and opportunities.

In summary, Susan Kenny's six elements—Information, Authenticity, Vision, Pragmatism, Strategy, and Transformation—provide a comprehensive framework for structuring community development work. Information ensures that efforts are evidence-based, Authenticity builds trust and credibility, Vision provides direction and motivation, Pragmatism balances idealism with practical realities, Strategy guides the implementation process, and Transformation seeks to achieve lasting and meaningful change. By integrating these elements, community development practitioners can design and execute initiatives that are both effective and aligned with the community's needs and aspirations.

4.5. Reflections and practical work sheets
What does 'Community development' actually mean?

As you embark on your journey into the field of community development, it's essential to delve into the core of what 'community development' truly means. Reflecting on this concept will help you grasp its multifaceted nature and its implications for practice. Here are some reflection questions to guide your understanding:

1. What are the core principles of community development, and how do they manifest in real-world scenarios?

Consider how principles such as empowerment, participation, and sustainability are applied in various community projects. Reflect on examples where these principles have led to tangible outcomes or where their absence has resulted in challenges.

2. How does community development differ from other forms of social change or intervention?

Reflect on the distinguishing features of community development compared to related fields such as social work, urban planning, or economic development. Think about what sets community development apart in terms of goals, methods, and impact.

3. In what ways does community development address the needs and aspirations of diverse communities?
Consider how community development approaches are tailored to fit the unique contexts, cultures, and needs of different communities. Reflect on the importance of cultural sensitivity and inclusivity in designing and implementing development initiatives.

4. What role does local leadership and community engagement play in the success of community development efforts?
Reflect on the importance of involving local leaders and community members in the planning and execution of development projects. Consider how their participation can influence the effectiveness and sustainability of the initiatives.

5. How can community development practitioners balance idealistic goals with practical constraints?
Think about the challenges of aligning ambitious community development goals with the practical realities of limited resources, political dynamics, and existing infrastructure. Reflect on strategies for managing these constraints while still striving for meaningful change.

6. What are some of the ethical considerations involved in community development work?
Reflect on the ethical dilemmas that practitioners might face, such as ensuring fairness, avoiding exploitation, and respecting the autonomy of community members. Consider how these ethical issues can impact the planning and execution of development projects.

7. How does the concept of community development evolve over time, and what are some emerging trends or challenges?
Consider how community development practices and theories have changed over time and what contemporary issues are shaping the field. Reflect on how new trends, such as technology and globalization, are influencing community development practices.

8. What are the indicators of successful community development, and how can they be measured?
Reflect on how success in community development is defined and measured. Consider what indicators might be used to evaluate the effectiveness of community development initiatives and how these measurements can guide future efforts.

9. How can personal values and perspectives influence your approach to community development?
Reflect on how your own values, experiences, and perspectives might shape your approach to community development. Consider how being aware of these influences can help you become a more effective and empathetic practitioner.

These reflection questions are designed to help you explore the depth and breadth of community development and to encourage a thoughtful examination of how this field operates and impacts the communities it serves. By engaging with these questions, you will develop a deeper understanding of community development and its critical role in fostering positive social change.

Figure 6 - Sample practical work sheets

- Activity Schedules

Activity Schedule	
Activity Type	Social engagement / Community Development/ Language School (Tamil/ Arabic/ Parsi)
Project:	

Who / What	When	Where

- Budget and expenditure template

Budget – Income and Expenditure	
Development activity	
Project:	

Income sources	Amount ($)
Grants	
In-kind contributions	
TOTAL INCOME	

Expenditure items	Income source	Amount ($)
TOTAL EXPENDITURE		

- Events Calender

Event Calendar	January				February				March				April				May				June			
	1	2	3	4	1	2	3	4	1	2	3	4	1	2	3	4	1	2	3	4	1	2	3	4
Press																								
Facebook																								
conducting sessions																								
Workshops																								
Event		█				█				█			█								█			
Post event PR		█																						
Closure of account & files																								

Strategy Planning			
Event name			
Contact Details		Name	Contact phone:
Action taken			
Organisation			
Brief overview			
-Completed projects /			
Community need			
Identified gap (Services required)			
Initiatives to address need			
List of current / proposed community-led activities or projects that address the community need. (Time-line / Budget and costing) - partnerships, External funding sources identified to support its delivery.			
A brief overview of the activity or project:			
Costs associated with delivery:			
Current or potential delivery partners:			
Services or funding that can support delivery:			

Community event planning

Community events planning encompasses a broad range of activities that require careful conceptualization and management to ensure successful execution. The process begins with the conceptualization of events, where planners identify the purpose, target audience, and overall objectives of the event. This initial stage sets the foundation for all subsequent planning and ensures that the event aligns with the community's needs and interests.

The SOST + 6 M Model is a valuable framework in this context, guiding planners through the critical stages of event management: Situation analysis, Objectives, Strategy, Tactics, Measurement, and Money. This model helps in developing a structured approach to planning, ensuring that each aspect of the event is thoroughly considered and addressed.

Cultural dimensions play a crucial role in event planning, especially in diverse communities. Planners must account for cultural differences in their approach, ensuring that events are inclusive and respectful of various traditions and practices. This involves understanding and integrating the cultural values, norms, and expectations of the community into the event's design and execution.

Various types of events, ranging from festivals and fairs to workshops and seminars, each require tailored planning strategies. Effective project planning and management are essential to coordinate these diverse event types, ensuring that every element—from logistics to staffing—is meticulously organized. This includes setting clear goals, developing timelines, and assigning responsibilities to ensure smooth execution.

Budgeting and financial management are critical components of event planning. Planners must develop a detailed budget that covers all potential expenses, from venue rentals to marketing costs. Financial oversight is necessary to manage costs effectively, secure funding, and ensure the event remains financially viable.

Marketing and promotions are key to attracting attendees and generating interest in the event. A strategic marketing plan should leverage various channels, including social media, local media, and community networks, to reach the target audience and maximize participation.

Despite careful planning, potential pitfalls can arise, such as logistical challenges, budget overruns, or insufficient community engagement. Identifying and addressing these risks in advance can help mitigate their impact, ensuring the event's success and achieving its objectives.

Overall, effective community event planning requires a

comprehensive approach that integrates conceptualization, cultural considerations, project management, budgeting, marketing, and risk management to create meaningful and successful events.

Brief overview -
- Conceptualizing Events
- SOST + 6 M Model
- Cultural Dimensions of events
- Types of events
- Effective Project planning & Management
- Budgeting and Financial Management
- Marketing & Promotions
- Potential Pitfalls

a) Conceptualizing Events
Conceptualizing community events involves defining the core purpose and objectives of the event to align with the needs and interests of the community. This initial stage focuses on understanding the goals, target audience, and desired outcomes, setting the foundation for all subsequent planning. It requires identifying key themes and activities that resonate with the community's cultural, social, and recreational preferences. Successful conceptualization integrates feedback from community members to ensure relevance and engagement, and lays out a clear vision for how the event will address specific needs or celebrate shared values. This thoughtful planning process is crucial for creating impactful and well-received community events.

b) SOST + 6 M Model

SOST – Situation, Objective, Strategy and Tactics

Situation: Assess the current environment and context of the event. Understand the needs, challenges, and opportunities within the community or market.

Objectives: Define clear, measurable goals for the event. Objectives should outline what the event aims to achieve, such as increasing community engagement, raising funds, or promoting a cause.

Strategy: Develop an overarching plan to achieve the objectives. This includes identifying key messages, target audiences, and the overall approach to organizing and executing the event.

Tactics: Detail the specific actions and methods required to implement the strategy. This covers logistical elements such as venue selection, scheduling, and staffing, as well as promotional activities.

6M Model

Manpower: Identify and allocate the necessary human resources for the event. This includes staffing, volunteers, and key roles required for planning and execution.

It is important to assess the skills required specially in a community development/ engagement

> **Men/Women/They**
> **The total manpower needed / skills required.**

Money: Develop and manage the event budget. This involves estimating costs, securing funding, monitoring expenses, and ensuring financial accountability.

> **Money**
> Venue cost, Transport, staging, Production, staff cost, support material etc.

Material: Determine and procure the physical resources needed for the event. This includes venue setup, equipment, supplies, and any other materials required for successful execution.

> **Material**
> Promotional material, brochures, stationery etc

Minutes: Establish a timeline and schedule for all event activities. This involves creating a detailed plan that outlines deadlines, milestones, and the sequence of tasks leading up to and during the event.

> **Minutes**
> Time required for planning and conducting the event

Machines / Methods: Plan and implement the processes and procedures for the event. This includes logistics, operational workflows, and the specific methods used to carry out various event functions efficiently.

Machines
Equipment required to carry the operation. Eg. AV, Lighting, Computers etc

Messages/ Measurement: Develop and deliver the communication strategy for the event. This involves creating promotional content, managing public relations, and ensuring clear and effective messaging to engage the target audience.

Measurements
Evaluation of achieving set targets

The 6 M model provides a comprehensive framework for organizing and managing all aspects of event planning, ensuring that every critical element is addressed for a successful outcome.

c) Cultural Dimensions of events

When planning events for Culturally and Linguistically Diverse (CaLD) communities in Western Australia, it is essential to consider several cultural dimensions to ensure inclusivity and respect for diverse backgrounds. Cultural sensitivity is paramount, requiring an understanding and respect for the various cultural practices, traditions, and values represented within these communities. This involves acknowledging and incorporating cultural norms and preferences into the event design to make sure all participants feel valued and represented.

Inclusivity plays a key role in this process. It is crucial to design events that are accessible to everyone, regardless of their cultural or linguistic background. This includes addressing practical considerations such as dietary restrictions, physical accessibility, and language barriers. Multilingual support, including interpreters and translated materials, can help bridge communication gaps and ensure that non-English speakers are fully able to participate.

Engaging with the community is also vital. Involving representatives from different cultural groups in the planning stages helps to ensure that the event aligns with their values and expectations. This collaboration fosters a sense of ownership and relevance among community members, enhancing their engagement and participation.

Cultural appropriateness must be maintained throughout the planning process. Event themes, activities, and content should be carefully chosen to avoid cultural insensitivity or misrepresentation. Consulting with cultural experts or community leaders can provide valuable insights and prevent potential issues.

Additionally, respecting religious and traditional observances is important. Event scheduling should take into account significant cultural or religious dates to avoid conflicts and show consideration for participants' practices.

Collaboration with the Office of Multicultural Interests can further support the planning process. This office can provide guidance on best practices for engaging with diverse communities and ensure that events align with broader multicultural policies and resources.

Finally, establishing feedback mechanisms allows for ongoing improvement. Gathering input from community members about their cultural needs and preferences helps to refine event planning and execution, ensuring that future events are even more inclusive and effective.

Incorporating these cultural dimensions ensures that events are meaningful, respectful, and engaging for Western Australia's diverse CaLD communities.

d) Types of events

Events in Culturally and Linguistically Diverse (CaLD) communities vary significantly based on the aims and objectives of the organizing groups. For instance, the Indian Society of Western Australia focuses on celebrating traditional festivals like Diwali and Holi, while the Organisation of African Communities of WA Inc. highlights diverse African cultures through music and dance festivals. Similarly, the Sri Lankan Cultural Society of Western Australia organizes events around traditional Sri Lankan holidays, whereas the WA Italian Club emphasizes Italian heritage through food and social gatherings, reflecting their distinct cultural priorities and community engagement goals.

In Western Australia, various types of community events organized by Culturally and Linguistically Diverse (CaLD) groups contribute significantly to the cultural richness and social fabric of the region. These events are hosted by a range of organizations, each bringing unique cultural perspectives and traditions to the broader community.

The Indian Society of Western Australia is known for hosting vibrant events that celebrate major Indian festivals such as Diwali, a festival of lights, and Holi, known for its colorful festivities. These events feature traditional music, dance, and cuisine, providing a rich cultural experience that showcases India's diverse heritage. The Society also organizes cultural workshops and educational programs to promote understanding and appreciation of Indian traditions.

The Organisation of African Communities of WA Inc. plays a crucial role in celebrating the diverse cultures of African nations. Their events include African cultural festivals that highlight traditional music, dance, and cuisine from various African regions. These festivals serve as a platform for the African community to share their cultural heritage with the wider public. Additionally, the Organization hosts support and community engagement events aimed at addressing issues relevant to African Australians, such as integration, education, and employment.

The Sri Lankan Cultural Society of Western Australia organizes events that reflect the rich traditions of Sri Lanka. Celebrations such as Sinhala and Tamil New Year are marked by traditional music, dance, and cuisine, offering an immersive cultural experience. The Society also hosts cultural performances and educational workshops to preserve and promote Sri Lankan heritage within the community.

The WA Italian Club is known for its celebration of Italian culture through events such as Italian festivals, food fairs, and social gatherings. These events often feature traditional Italian cuisine, music, and dance, providing a festive atmosphere that celebrates Italian heritage and fosters community spirit.

The Nepali Association of WA organizes events that highlight Nepali traditions and cultural practices. Celebrations such as Dashain and Tihar, major Nepali festivals, are marked by traditional rituals, music, and dance. The Association also holds community gatherings and cultural workshops to promote understanding of Nepali customs and support the Nepali diaspora in Western Australia.

The Castellorizian Association of WA focuses on celebrating the heritage of Castellorizo, a Greek island. Their events often include traditional Greek music, dance, and cuisine, reflecting the cultural traditions of Castellorizo. The Association's activities aim to preserve and share Greek cultural practices with the broader community.

The Burmese Association of WA organizes events that celebrate Burmese culture and traditions. These include cultural festivals that showcase traditional Burmese music, dance, and food, offering a glimpse into the rich heritage of Burma (Myanmar). The Association also hosts community events that address the needs of Burmese Australians and promote cultural exchange.

Each of these organizations contributes to a vibrant and diverse community landscape in Western Australia by hosting events that celebrate their unique cultural heritages. These events not only strengthen community bonds but also offer opportunities for intercultural understanding and appreciation among the wider population. Through their diverse programs, these organizations play a crucial role in enriching Western Australia's multicultural society.

The diversity in event types across Culturally and Linguistically Diverse (CaLD) communities underscores the importance of aligning event planning with the specific objectives of each organization. By carefully considering the aims and cultural priorities of the organizing groups, planners can create events that genuinely reflect and celebrate the unique heritage and values of the communities they serve. Tailoring event planning to these objectives ensures that each event is not only meaningful and engaging but also effectively fulfills its purpose, fostering greater cultural understanding and community cohesion.

e) Effective Project planning & Management

Effective project planning and management are crucial for the success of community organizations, as they ensure that initiatives are executed efficiently and meet their intended goals. In the context of community organizations, which often operate with limited resources and diverse stakeholder interests, meticulous planning is essential for aligning project objectives with community needs. This involves setting clear goals, developing detailed timelines, and coordinating resources and personnel to achieve desired outcomes. By employing robust project management strategies, community organizations can navigate complexities, optimize their efforts, and deliver impactful programs that strengthen community ties and address local challenges.

Sample Event management Plan

Planning is the most important part of delivering a successful event. An Events Management Plan (EMP) will help you to establish clear responsibilities, ensure you meet legal responsibilities, and identify and manage foreseeable risks.

This template will assist you to identify and plan for the multiple facets of an event. It is intended as a guide only and <u>may not cover all components</u> of your event – each event is different, and each will have activities and features that need to be considered in an EMP.

Consult with the local council for more details.

Most venues can now be booked online through user-friendly platforms that streamline the reservation process, eliminating the need for manual site visits. These platforms often provide virtual tours, detailed layouts, and booking tools that allow users to select and secure their desired space with ease.

1. Event Details

Event Name	
Type of Event	Community/ Commercial/ Sporting/School/ Fundraiser-Charity
Purpose of event	(ie. why do you want to hold the event?)
Date/s	
Location	
Expected Number of Attendees	
Is the event ticketed	Yes No

Participants	Spectators	Volunteers

Event Description

Event Description (e.g., type of event, target audience, event highlights and entertainment)	

Event Organiser's Details

Event Organiser	
Organisation/Committee	
Contact Phone Number	
Email Address	
Postal Address	

Event Personnel

List the key roles of Event Staff/Volunteers, the role description, and the role responsibilities.

(eg. Event Manager, Medical/First Aid Co-ordinator, Site Manager, Food Stall co-ordinator, Emergency/Evacuation Warden, Traffic Marshals, Treasurer/Money Handler, Market Stall & Amusements Co-ordinator, Security/Crowd Control Marshals etc).

Role Title	Role Description	Role Responsibilities
Eg. Co-ordinator of Volunteers	Oversee the event volunteers	Recruit, train, induct and co-ordinate volunteers
Security officer	Crowd control	To monitor crowd, deal with anti-social behaviour, contact police if necessary and complete incident reports.
	Insert additional rows in table as needed	

Event Schedule

Include the bump in/out dates and times for the venue and any major events/activities during the event.

Date/Time	Activity
e.g. 01/01/2021	Bump In
6.00am	Staff arrive on site.
8.00am	Contractor arriving for XXX
	Insert additional rows in table as needed

2. Event Requirements
2.1 Site Map
Attach your event site plan to this document.

Site plan attached	Yes No

Check List
- Surrounding roads
- Car parking
- Emergency exits.
- Emergency assembly areas
- First aid location/s
- Stall locations
- Stage/temporary structures
- Amenities (toilets)
- Bins
- Water

![assembly]	Evacuation assembly area
![first aid]	First aid
![info]	Information
![marquee]	Marquee (include dimensions)
![stage]	Stage (include dimensions)
![seating]	Seating
![food]	Food/beverage vendor
![toilets]	Toilets (include amount and M/F/AA (male, female, all access))
![bins]	Bins (equal number of general waste & recycling required)
![water]	Drinking water
![fire]	Fire extinguisher
![parking]	Car parking
![power]	Power / Generators

Most venues can now be booked online through user-friendly platforms that streamline the reservation process, eliminating the need for manual site visits. These platforms often provide virtual tours, detailed layouts, and booking tools that allow users to select and secure their desired space with ease. Consequently, the requirement for drawing site maps has diminished, as digital tools offer comprehensive visual and logistical information to facilitate efficient event planning.

2.2 Risk Assessment

If required by the Council / Local authorities - attach your completed Risk Assessment to this document. A Risk Assessment must be completed prior to the event and should identify, assess, and control all risks relevant to the event.

All risks have been identified	Yes No
Risk assessment attached	Yes No

2.3 Public Liability

Attach a copy of your Public Liability Insurance Certificate with this document. Public liability insurance must include Insurer details, date of cover, amount of cover (no less than $20 million)

Public Liability Insurance Certificate attached	Yes No

Who (role title) will ensure that appropriate insurance is in place (eg. Public Liability, Product Liability, Property Liability etc), that the level of insurance is adequate and that all activities will be covered?

How will this be done?

2.4 Traffic Management Plan (if applicable)

Where an event is likely to affect traffic conditions or require a temporary road closure on any Council roads, or State Government roads, organisers are required to seek approval from the Traffic Committee

Attach Transport Management Plan and any relevant Traffic Control Permits (if applicable) to this document if this is required for your event.

Transport Management Plan attached	Yes No N/A

2.5 Notification Plan

To minimise any impact on surrounding residents and businesses you are required to notify and consult with the community and businesses located near to your event.

A formal letter must be sent to all stakeholders within the event precinct at least 30 prior to the event. The Events Team can help you develop a list of who should be targeted directly and identify the areas and streets to be included in your distribution.

Your letter must be on your official letterhead and include the following details:

- the name, date, and location of your event (including bump-in and bump-out times)
- the purpose of the event
- the expected number of attendees
- activities being conducted as part of the event.
- what the likely disruptions to residents and businesses will be with respect to noise, transport, and road closures
- a contact number (before and during the event) for further information or queries

How will you advise the community? (i.e., letterbox drop, social media posts etc.)	
Will you be using VMS boards?	Yes No
When will you notify the community?	
Additional details/comment	
Map of notification area (attached)	Yes No

3. Public Health

3.1 Food Vendors

Provide a list of food vendors (both temporary food stalls, mobile food vehicles, caterers etc). You will also be required to check each food vendor holds a current Food Business License and ensure a copy of their current certificate is provided to Council prior to the event (certificate must also be displayed at each stall).

Business Trading Name	Contact Number	Type of license (i.e. temporary food stall, mobile food vehicle etc)
e.g. Indian Curry van	*04XX XXX XXX*	*Mobile Food Van*
		Insert additional rows in table as needed

3.2 Alcohol

Provide information relating to alcohol being sold/served at the event. You will need to provide a copy of your Liquor License (where applicable).

Will alcohol be at the event?	Yes No
Has the liquor license been attached?	Yes No N/A
Additional details/comments	

3.3 Toilet Facilities

Provide details on the number of toilets that will be available or supplied at the event. Toilets must be provided with soap, running water and paper towels.

Amenity Type	Number of toilets
Male	
Female	
Disabled	
All toilets provided with hand washing (including soap and paper towel)?	Yes No
Toilets marked on site map	Yes No

3.4 Cleaning and Sanitising

Provide details on how the facilities and event grounds will be cleaned and serviced during/after the event.

Will a cleaning roster/procedure be implemented for the event?	Yes No
Provide details (i.e. external cleaning contractor or event staff, cleaning and sanitising methods and frequency).	

3.5 Water Supply

Provide information on water supply that will be made available at the event e.g. will there be an adequate supply of potable water for drinking?

Will there be potable (drinking) water be at the event?	Yes No
Provide details	

3.6 Waste Management

Provide information on the number of general waste and recycling bins that will be at the event. Provide the waste contractor's details and how waste will be handled/disposed of during and after the event.

Waste contractor/s details			
No. General waste bins	No. Recycle bins		No. Skip bins
Bins marked on site map	Yes No		

3.7 Environmental Impact

While conducting the event you must take all reasonable and practical measures to minimise environmental impacts and nuisances to the surrounding community and businesses.

Provide information on the activities that are likely to cause a nuisance during the event (such as noise from music) or an environmental impact (such as spills or waste that require clean up) and address how these will be monitored, minimised, or controlled.

Type of impact	Likely to occur	Details
Noise (i.e. music, PA announcer etc)	Yes No N/A	
Obtrusive lighting	Yes No N/A	
Dust/fumes/smoke	Yes No N/A	
Liquid spills or waste requiring clean up	Yes No N/A	
	Yes No N/A	Insert additional rows in table as needed

4. Safety

4.1 First Aid

It is the organisers responsibility to provide a safe and healthy environment for those attending and working at their event.

Provide details of the first aid provisions that will be available at the event. Include information on the number of first aid personnel, first aid posts and qualifications.

Number of first aid stations	
Details of first aid officer/s (include company and individual name)	Are they qualified?
	Yes No
Insert additional rows in table as needed	Yes No

4.2 Incident Reporting

During the event it is important to make a record of incidents and near misses that occur. These should be logged in a format that includes date & time of incident, description of what occurred, person involved, and action taken.

Will incidents and near misses be reported?	Yes No
Provide details on how these will be reported (i.e. what method will be used for reporting).	

4.3 Signage (inside the event)

Ensure applicable signage is displayed inside the event for safety and communication to attendees. Provide information on signage that will be installed.

Signage	Provided	Details
Entry/Exit	Yes No	
Information Point	Yes No	
First Aid Location/s	Yes No	
Toilets	Yes No	
Drinking Water	Yes No	
		Insert additional rows in table as needed

4.4 Power Supply

Provide a description of the power supply for the event. Information should include if the supply is from a generator or another source.

Will power be needed at the event?	Yes No
Detail how this will be supplied (i.e. power from venue or generator, will a licensed electrician be conducting the work).	

4.5 Lighting (if applicable)

Provide information on the lighting that will be provided at the event. If your event is in the evening, consider lighting that may be necessary to ensure safety of attendees at the event and entering/exiting the event.

Will sufficient lighting be at the event to ensure safety?	Yes No N/A
Detail the type of lighting that will be installed (ensure this is included on your site map also).	

5. Emergency Response Plan
5.1 Primary Contact

The Primary Contact is the person who acts as the main contact person for the Organisation/Event in an emergency. The Primary Contact is responsible for making decisions and following the steps described in this emergency response plan. A Secondary Contact is required to act as the Primary Contact if they become unavailable.

Primary Contact	Secondary Contact
Name:	Name:
Contact No:	Contact No:

5.2 Emergency Contacts
PRIMARY EMERGENCY CONTACT Dial 000

Police	Fire
Local Station:	Local Station:
Contact:	Contact:
Number:	Number:
SES	Local Hospital
Emergency No:	Name:
Contact:	Address:
Number:	Number:
On-site First Aid Provider	On-site Security
Provider Name:	Provider Name:
On-site Contact Person:	On-site Contact Person:
Number:	Number
Other	Other

Police Notification

It is the responsibility of the Event Organiser to notify the Police of any event or public gathering well in advance of its occurrence. This notification should be carried out by completing a Public Assembly Notice form as stipulated by the Public Meetings and Processions Act 1984 (WA). The Western Australian Police Force (WAPOL) will review the application and may issue a permit in accordance with Section 7 of the Public Order in Streets Act 1984. The form can be accessed via the Western Australian Police Force website.

Additionally, if the event takes place in or passes through privately managed public spaces, it is crucial to inform and consult directly with the respective managers to address any specific requirements they may have.

For events at Parliament House, contact receptionservices@parliament.wa.gov.au.

For the Perth Cultural Centre, email pccevents@ptt.wa.gov.au

For Elizabeth Quay, reach out to elizabethquay@cbre.com.au

and for Yagan Square, contact yagan@cbre.com.au

Ensuring timely and effective communication with these entities is essential for compliance and successful event management.

5.4 Evacuation Procedure

In the event of an emergency or incident that requires an evacuation, describe the details and procedures of how an evacuation would be conducted. Ensure emergency evacuation routes mentioned in your procedure are included on your site plan.

5.3 Communications Plan

In the event of an emergency, clear and effective communication is paramount to ensure the safety and coordination of all parties involved. Communication with the event team, emergency services, and attendees will be managed primarily through a combination of radio systems and mobile phones, ensuring that critical information is relayed promptly. A Public Address (PA) system will be utilized to broadcast emergency instructions to attendees, maintaining a clear line of communication with the public.

Should these primary communication systems fail, alternate

arrangements will be activated. In the absence of mobile coverage, designated team members will use two-way radios with backup batteries to maintain contact and coordinate responses. Additionally, pre-established emergency procedures will include the use of visual signals, such as flags or hand signals, to facilitate communication when electronic systems are compromised. These measures are designed to ensure that emergency protocols can be effectively executed, safeguarding both attendees and staff under any circumstances.

5.4 Contingency plan / Wet weather plan
If applicable, A contingency plan should be in place in case the event needs to be cancelled or moved due to rain, extreme weather or unforeseen circumstances (eg. Covid, illness etc)

How will impacted persons be notified if the event is being cancelled or moved to an alternate location? (keep in mind different methods of notification may be required for different stakeholders, eg event committee, participants/stall holders, attendees, Council)

Who (role title) will oversee the notifications?	Response
Will the event proceed at an alternate location if it is unable to be held at the nominated location due to adverse weather? If yes, consider the following:	Name of the alternate location - Applies to AGM's / Committee meeting / power outage

Who (role title) will contact Council to determine the condition and/or status of the event site if heavy rain/adverse weather conditions are experienced in the lead up to the event?	

5.5 Lost Children / Lost and stolen property procedure

It is important to plan for lost children including providing an area where lost children can be looked after and where carers can find them.

Provide details of the Lost Child procedure to be followed during the event.

(a) Who (role title) will handle occurrences involving lost children and/or property?	(b) Provide details on how this will be managed

5.6 Preparation and Training

Induction
(a) Who (role title) will co-ordinate the induction and briefing of event personnel, volunteers and, where relevant, participants (eg: Cricket Carnivals/ Athletic/ Cultural events)?

When/where will induction sessions be held?

Location	Date & Time	Inductee/ Group

Describe what the induction/briefing sessions will cover

Security

Who (role title) will determine the level of security that will be required at the event, and co-ordinate/engage?

<u>If you are engaging security personnel at your event (eg police or uniformed security guards)</u>:

Provide details on numbers, locations and duties of any security personnel:

Detail how incidents will be dealt with:

<u>If no security personnel will be engaged</u>:
Who (role title) will be responsible for managing anti-social behaviour, the safe keeping of cash on-site, and incidents of damaged or stolen equipment/infrastructure?

How will this be done? How will incidents be dealt with?

Sponsorship & Event partners (Other than Council)
Is your event sponsored by party/s other than Council?
Yes? Complete questions below
No? Go to the next section
Note: Sometimes council requires details of all sponsors, proposed sponsors and/or event partners to ensure that no conflict of interest exists and to determine that sponsors are appropriate to the event and/or community.

If the event is being sponsored by parties other than Council, please provide the names of all contributing persons/organisations

6. Post Event Evaluations

Interim Indicators		Experimental Indicators	
Activity	No. of Items	On-going Changes	Units
- Workshops		Membership Increase	
- External Participation		Member achievements	
- Community Activities		Member requests	

Figure 6 - Sample practical work sheets

4.6. Summary

Community development is a multifaceted field focused on enhancing the quality of life within communities through collective efforts and strategic planning. Its concepts and literature emphasize various approaches to empower communities, foster social cohesion, and address local needs.

At its core, community development is grounded in principles of participation, equity, and sustainability. It involves engaging local residents in identifying their needs, resources, and aspirations, and then collaboratively developing strategies to address them. This participatory approach is crucial for ensuring that development efforts are responsive to the unique contexts and desires of different communities.

Useful Websites

1. Australian Community Workers Association (ACWA)
Overview: Provides resources, professional development, and accreditation for community workers in Australia. It also offers insights into community development practices and standards.
Website: https://www.acwa.org.au/

2. Australian Government – Department of Social Services (DSS)
Overview: Offers information on various community development programs and funding opportunities managed by the Australian Government. Useful for accessing policy updates and government resources.
Website: https://www.dss.gov.au/

3. Community Council for Australia (CCA)
Overview: Focuses on strengthening the community sector through advocacy, support, and policy development. It provides useful reports, research, and tools for community organizations.
Website: https://communitycouncil.org.au/

4. Australian Institute of Family Studies (AIFS)
Overview: Conducts research and provides resources on family and community issues, including community development practices and impacts.
Website: https://aifs.gov.au/

5. Victorian Council of Social Service (VCOSS)
Overview: Provides advocacy, research, and policy advice on social issues, including community development in Victoria. It offers

valuable insights and resources for community-based organizations.
Website: https://vcoss.org.au/

CHAPTER 5

FRAMEWORK FOR WORKING WITH COMMUNITIES

5.1. Introduction

This chapter delves into essential frameworks for working with communities, focusing on participatory action research (PAR) and the principles of participative democracy. These frameworks offer structured approaches to engage communities effectively, ensuring that development efforts are both inclusive and impactful.

- Building an evidence base in community engagement and social interaction development
- Considering the two elements to democracy – Representative and Participative democracy
- Define the '**Participatory Action Research' (PAR)**

a. Overview of PAR

Participatory Action Research (PAR) is a collaborative research methodology that empowers communities to actively participate in the research process. This section introduces PAR as a dynamic framework that integrates research with action, aiming to address local issues through collective inquiry and problem-solving. It emphasizes the importance of community involvement in every stage of the research—from identifying problems to implementing solutions.

b. Key Principles of PAR

The chapter outlines the core principles of PAR, including collaboration, reflection, and iterative learning. It highlights how PAR fosters an environment where community members and researchers work together to generate knowledge and effect change. By prioritizing the voices and perspectives of those directly affected by the issues, PAR ensures that research outcomes are relevant and actionable.

c. Practical Applications of PAR

This section explores real-world applications of PAR, including forming research partnerships, collecting and analyzing data, and translating findings into practical interventions. The chapter provides insights into how PAR can lead to tangible improvements and enhanced community well-being.

5.1.1. Building an evidence base

As community engagement practitioners, our role extends beyond implementing programs and initiatives; it involves developing a nuanced understanding of community dynamics and ensuring our efforts are grounded in a robust evidence-base. The Aspen Institute, as articulated by Auspos and Kubisch (2004), highlights the necessity of deepening our inquiry into fundamental questions about community development, drawing from a diverse range of evidence sources, and expanding our knowledge base beyond traditional program evaluations. This approach is crucial for fostering meaningful and sustainable community impact.

To build a comprehensive evidence-base, we must first recognize that traditional evaluations—while valuable for assessing program outputs and immediate outcomes—often fall short of capturing the full spectrum of community dynamics and the nuanced impacts of our initiatives. Formal evaluations typically focus on quantitative metrics such as participation rates and immediate changes in behavior or conditions. While these metrics provide important information, they may not fully capture the underlying causes of community issues, the lived experiences of community members, or the longer-term effects of interventions.

Auspos and Kubisch advocate for a richer, more holistic approach to evidence collection. This involves incorporating qualitative data, which can offer profound insights into how community members experience and perceive interventions. For instance, interviews, focus groups, and participatory workshops allow us to gather personal stories and feedback, which are critical for understanding the real-world impact of our work. These qualitative insights can reveal issues and successes that quantitative data alone might overlook, such as changes in community cohesion or shifts in local attitudes.

Moreover, contextual information plays a crucial role in building a comprehensive evidence-base. Understanding the broader socio-economic and cultural context of a community helps us design and implement interventions that are truly responsive to local needs. This means examining local history, social structures, and existing resources, which can inform how we approach development efforts and ensure they are tailored to the community's unique characteristics.

Another important aspect is process data, which involves documenting and analyzing how interventions are implemented. This includes examining the processes involved, how community members engage with these processes, and any adjustments made along the way. Process data helps us understand the dynamics of implementation and identify factors that contribute to or hinder the success of our initiatives.

To develop a more comprehensive knowledge base, we need to address several key questions as suggested by Auspos and Kubisch. One crucial question is identifying the underlying causes of community issues. This involves digging deeper into the root causes rather than just addressing surface-level symptoms. By understanding these root causes, we can design interventions that address systemic issues and create more lasting change.

Another important question is how community members experience and perceive our interventions. Gathering qualitative feedback from those directly affected allows us to gauge the true impact of our efforts and make necessary adjustments. This feedback helps ensure that our initiatives are not only effective but also aligned with the community's needs and values.

Additionally, examining the long-term effects of community initiatives is essential. Short-term outcomes are important, but understanding how interventions sustain their impact over time provides valuable insights into their effectiveness and longevity. This perspective helps us refine our approaches and enhance the sustainability of our efforts.

Expanding our evidence-base also means drawing on diverse sources of information. Local knowledge is a valuable resource, as engaging with community members, local experts, and stakeholders provides insights that may not be captured through formal evaluations alone. Their perspectives can shed light on community strengths, challenges, and potential solutions.

Academic research and theories related to community development should also inform our practice. By integrating existing research, we can align our interventions with proven strategies and theoretical frameworks, thereby enhancing their effectiveness. Additionally, analyzing case studies of both successful and unsuccessful community initiatives can offer practical lessons and best practices that are applicable to our own work.

Creating a learning environment is essential for applying and expanding our knowledge base. Establishing feedback mechanisms allows community members and stakeholders to share their experiences and suggestions regularly. Knowledge sharing through workshops, conferences, and online platforms encourages the exchange of ideas and experiences among practitioners, researchers, and community members. This collaborative approach fosters continuous learning and adaptation.

Incorporating evidence into practice involves designing interventions based on the insights gathered from our expanded evidence-base. This means using qualitative feedback, contextual information, and process data to shape our strategies and ensure they are responsive to community needs. Developing a comprehensive monitoring and evaluation framework that includes both quantitative and qualitative indicators allows us to track progress and make data-informed adjustments.

Effectively communicating the evidence and impact of our work is also crucial. Detailed reports that present evidence in an accessible and actionable format, combined with narratives and case studies that illustrate real-world impacts, help engage stakeholders and secure support for community development efforts. Advocating for evidence-based approaches within the community and among decision-makers reinforces the value of our work and helps garner the necessary resources and backing.

In summary, building a robust evidence-base for community development requires a shift from traditional evaluation methods to a more holistic and inclusive approach. By addressing key questions, drawing on diverse sources of evidence, and fostering a culture of continuous learning, we can enhance the effectiveness and sustainability of our interventions, ultimately leading to more meaningful and lasting community impact.

5.2. Participative democracy

As community engagement practitioners, developing a robust evidence-base is fundamental to ensuring that our initiatives are both effective and responsive to the needs of the communities we serve. A critical component of this endeavor involves understanding and applying the principles of representative and participative democracy. Research by Ife and Tesoriero (2006) highlights that while representative democracy is an essential aspect of governance, it is not sufficient on its own for effective community development. Instead, it must be complemented by participative democracy to truly achieve good governance.

Representative Democracy and Its Limitations
Representative democracy, where elected officials make decisions on behalf of the populace, is a cornerstone of modern governance. It provides a structured mechanism for people to have their voices heard through their representatives. However, Ife and Tesoriero (2006) argue that representative democracy alone does not necessarily equate to good governance. This approach can sometimes create a disconnect between the needs and concerns of the community and the decisions made by those in power. Elected representatives may not always have the capacity to fully understand or address the complexities of local issues without direct input from the community.

The Need for Participative Democracy
To bridge this gap, participative democracy is essential. Participative democracy involves the active involvement of community members in decision-making processes, ensuring that their voices are directly incorporated into governance. According to Ife and Tesoriero, this approach allows for a more nuanced understanding of community needs and fosters greater accountability and transparency. It ensures that the policies and initiatives developed are more reflective of the community's actual needs and aspirations.

In practice, participative democracy can take various forms, such as community forums, advisory committees, and collaborative decision-making processes. These mechanisms enable community members to engage directly with decision-makers, contribute their perspectives, and influence the direction of policies and programs. By integrating participative democracy, we create a more inclusive and responsive governance structure that enhances the legitimacy and effectiveness of community initiatives.

Challenges in Larger Agencies

However, integrating participative democracy becomes increasingly challenging as agencies and organizations grow in size and complexity. Larger agencies often face difficulties in maintaining meaningful engagement with all stakeholders. The hierarchical nature and bureaucratic processes typical of large organizations can create barriers to effective participation. These challenges can lead to a situation where community engagement becomes tokenistic or superficial, rather than genuinely impactful.

To address these challenges, it is crucial for larger agencies to adopt strategies that facilitate meaningful participation despite their size. This might involve decentralizing decision-making processes to allow for more localized input or using technology to enhance engagement opportunities. For example, digital platforms can provide a means for broader and more inclusive participation, enabling community members to contribute their views and feedback efficiently.

Building a Comprehensive Evidence-Base – (Re-iterating 5.1.1. Building an evidence base)

Incorporating participative democracy into community development efforts also requires a commitment to building a comprehensive evidence-base. This involves not only gathering quantitative data on program outcomes but also integrating qualitative insights from community members. By employing participative methods such as surveys, focus groups, and participatory action research, practitioners can gain a deeper understanding of the impact of their initiatives and the experiences of those they serve.

Furthermore, it is essential to continuously assess and adapt governance structures to ensure they support effective community engagement. This includes evaluating the effectiveness of participative mechanisms, addressing any barriers to participation, and making adjustments based on feedback and evolving community needs. By doing so, we can create a governance model that is both representative and participative, ensuring that community development efforts are informed by a rich and diverse evidence-base.

Research inference
Inferencing the qualitative and quantitative research, while representative democracy is a foundational element of governance, it must be complemented by participative democracy to achieve truly effective community development. As Ife and Tesoriero (2006) emphasize, the integration of participative practices helps bridge the gap between decision-makers and the community, fostering more responsive and accountable governance. For larger agencies, overcoming the challenges associated with scaling participative democracy requires innovative approaches and a commitment to genuine engagement. By building a comprehensive evidence-base that includes both quantitative and qualitative data, and by continuously adapting governance structures to support meaningful participation, community engagement practitioners can enhance the effectiveness and impact of their initiatives.

5.3. Practice framework for integrative partnerships
In the realm of community engagement, employing a structured approach to research and evidence collection is crucial for developing initiatives that are both effective and reflective of community needs. Participatory Action Research (PAR) provides a robust

framework for this purpose, offering a process that ensures research is deeply integrated with community involvement. Drawing on Stinger's (1999) principles of PAR, we can outline a detailed practice framework for integrating partnerships and building a comprehensive evidence-base for community development.

i) Starting Out: Defining the Initial Question

The journey begins with formulating a starting question. This initial question should stem from a genuine concern or issue identified within the community. It is essential that this question reflects the community's own priorities and challenges, rather than being imposed from external sources. This initial inquiry sets the stage for the entire research process and ensures that the subsequent steps are grounded in real and relevant issues.

ii) Designing the Research

Once the starting question is established, the next step is to design the research. This involves deciding on the methodologies and approaches that will best address the question. Participatory Action Research emphasizes collaborative design, meaning that community members should be actively involved in shaping the research process. This co-design approach helps ensure that the research methods are culturally appropriate, practical, and tailored to the community's context.

iii) Seeking Information from Other Communities

Before diving into primary data collection, it is valuable to seek information from other communities that have faced similar issues. This background research can provide insights into effective strategies and potential pitfalls, offering a broader perspective that informs the local research design. Learning from the experiences of other communities helps refine the approach and adapt successful practices to the local context.

iv) Refining the Question

With initial insights from other communities in hand, the next step is to refine the starting question. This iterative process involves revisiting and honing the question based on new knowledge and insights. Refining the question ensures that it remains focused and relevant, incorporating any new understanding gained from secondary research and initial discussions with community members.

V) Collecting Information

At this stage, the research moves into the data collection phase. This involves gathering information directly from the community through various methods such as surveys, interviews, focus groups, and observations. It is crucial that this process is conducted in a manner that is inclusive and respectful, allowing all voices within the community to be heard. The data collected at this stage provides a foundational understanding of the issue at hand.

vi) Refining the Question Again

As data is collected, it often becomes apparent that further refinement of the question is necessary. This iterative refinement ensures that the research question evolves in response to the findings, allowing for a deeper exploration of the issue. This step may involve adjusting the focus to address emerging themes or new insights that have come to light through initial data collection.

vii) Collecting More Information

With the refined question, additional data collection is conducted. This phase aims to fill any gaps identified during the earlier stages and to further explore the nuances of the issue. The iterative nature of PAR means that data collection is not a one-time event but a continuous process that adapts based on ongoing findings.

viii) Making Sense of the Information

After collecting sufficient data, the next step is to make sense of the information. This involves analyzing and interpreting the data to draw meaningful conclusions. The goal is to understand patterns, trends, and insights that can inform the development of effective interventions. In participatory research, this analysis is often conducted collaboratively with community members to ensure that the interpretations align with their perspectives and experiences.

ix) Checking the Findings with Community Members

It is essential to validate the findings with the community to ensure accuracy and relevance. This step involves presenting the analyzed data back to the community for feedback and validation. Engaging community members in this process helps to verify that the findings truly reflect their experiences and concerns. It also fosters transparency and builds trust, ensuring that the research process remains grounded in community engagement.

x) Putting It into Practice

The final step is to put the findings into practice. This involves translating the insights gained from the research into actionable strategies and interventions. It is important to communicate the outcomes and recommendations clearly to the community and relevant stakeholders. Effective dissemination of the findings ensures that the research leads to tangible improvements and informs future actions.

In conclusion, adopting Stinger's (1999) principles of Participatory Action Research offers a comprehensive framework for building an evidence-base in community development. By following a structured process that emphasizes iterative questioning, collaborative design, and community validation, practitioners can ensure that their research is both rigorous and deeply connected to the needs and experiences of the community. This approach not only enhances the effectiveness of interventions but also strengthens the partnership between researchers and community members, leading to more sustainable and impactful outcomes.

'Action research' framework – Do not tie community groups to pre-determined outcomes

In community engagement, ensuring that projects are both accountable and responsive to the needs of the community is paramount. 'Action Research' or 'Action Learning' offer valuable frameworks for developing community projects that do not confine groups to pre-determined outcomes. These methodologies emphasize collaboration, flexibility, and continuous learning, allowing for projects that evolve in response to real-time feedback and emerging needs.

Understanding Action Research and Action Learning

Action Research or Action Learning are iterative, participatory approaches designed to address complex issues through collaborative problem-solving and reflection. Action Research involves a cycle of planning, acting, observing, and reflecting, allowing for continuous adaptation based on the insights gained during the project. Action Learning, on the other hand, focuses on learning from real-life problems through action and reflection, emphasizing the development of practical solutions and personal growth.

Framework for Developing Accountable Projects

The key to developing accountable projects with these frameworks is to create an environment where community input drives decision-making processes and outcomes are not predetermined. Here's how you can implement these principles effectively:

1. Initiating the Process with Community Engagement

Begin by engaging with the community to identify their needs, concerns, and aspirations. This initial engagement should be open-ended, allowing community members to articulate their views and priorities without being constrained by pre-defined objectives. The goal is to develop a shared understanding of the issues at hand and to collaboratively explore potential areas for intervention.

2. Co-Designing the Project

Once the community's needs are understood, co-design the project with active participation from community members. This collaborative design process ensures that the project reflects the community's input and is tailored to address their specific context. By involving community members in the planning stages, you create a sense of ownership and commitment to the project.

3. Implementing Iterative Planning and Action

Adopt an iterative approach to project implementation, where planning and action occur in cycles. Begin with a small-scale pilot or initial phase of the project, allowing for experimentation and adaptation. During each cycle, collect feedback from the community and assess the effectiveness of the interventions. This iterative process enables adjustments to be made based on real-time insights, ensuring that the project remains relevant and responsive to changing conditions.

4. Reflecting and Learning

Incorporate regular reflection and learning sessions into the project framework. These sessions should involve both project team members and community stakeholders. Use these opportunities to evaluate what is working well, identify challenges, and gather insights on how to improve the project. Action Research and Action Learning emphasize the importance of reflection in learning from experiences and making informed adjustments.

5. Ensuring Flexibility in Outcomes

One of the core principles of Action Research and Action Learning is to avoid tying projects to pre-determined outcomes. Instead, focus on creating flexible objectives that can evolve based on ongoing feedback and learning. This approach allows the project to adapt to new information and changing circumstances, ensuring that the outcomes are not rigidly predefined but are instead shaped by the community's evolving needs.

6. Building Accountability through Transparency

Maintain transparency throughout the project by regularly communicating progress and findings to the community. Share updates on what has been achieved, what challenges have been encountered, and how the project is being adapted in response to feedback. This transparency fosters trust and ensures that the community remains engaged and informed about the project's direction.

7. Evaluating and Adapting

At each stage of the project, conduct evaluations that focus on both process and outcomes. Assess how well the project is meeting the community's needs and whether the interventions are having the desired impact. Use these evaluations to make necessary adjustments and to inform future phases of the project. The emphasis on ongoing evaluation and adaptation aligns with the principles of Action Research and Action Learning, ensuring that the project remains dynamic and effective.

8. Documenting and Sharing Lessons Learned

Document the lessons learned throughout the project and share these insights with the community and other stakeholders. This documentation not only provides valuable information for future projects but also reinforces the collaborative nature of the process. By sharing experiences and outcomes, you contribute to a broader knowledge base that can benefit other community engagement efforts.

Application in community settings

By applying the principles of Action Research and Action Learning, community engagement practitioners can develop accountable projects that are flexible, responsive, and grounded in real-time feedback. This approach ensures that projects are not constrained by pre-determined outcomes but are instead shaped by the evolving needs and input of the community. Through iterative planning, collaborative design, ongoing reflection, and transparent communication, practitioners can foster more effective and sustainable community development efforts.

Figure 7 - Piggot- Irvine's action research model

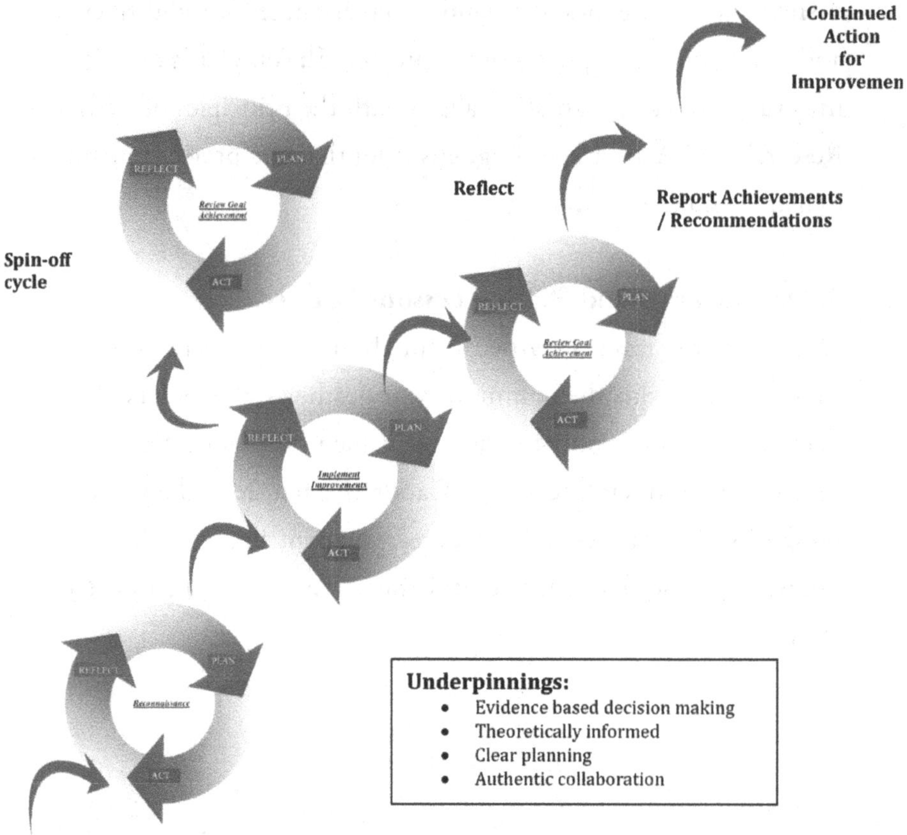
Continued Action for Improvemen
Reflect
Report Achievements / Recommendations
Spin-off cycle
REFLECT
PLAN
ACT
REFLECT
PLAN
ACT
REFLECT
PLAN
ACT
REFLECT
PLAN
ACT
Underpinnings:
Evidence based decision making
Theoretically informed
Clear planning
Authentic collaboration

5.4. Roles – Getting it clear

As a community engagement practitioner, defining and performing your role effectively involves a thoughtful approach to crafting a role statement, a mission statement, and understanding the interplay between the circle of concern and the circle of influence. These elements are crucial for guiding your actions, aligning with broader goals, and strategically focusing your efforts to maximize impact.

The Role Statement

A role statement articulates the specific responsibilities, expectations, and functions associated with your position as a community engagement practitioner. It serves as a comprehensive guide that outlines what is expected in your role and how you are expected to contribute to the community's development.

Creating a role statement involves several steps. Begin by identifying the core functions of your role, which might include facilitating community meetings, coordinating outreach efforts, developing and implementing programs, and fostering partnerships. The role statement should clearly describe these functions, detailing the scope of responsibilities, the goals to be achieved, and the methods to be employed. For instance, a role statement might outline your responsibility to engage with diverse community groups, assess their needs, and collaborate with local stakeholders to develop tailored interventions.

The role statement also helps in setting clear expectations for both you and the community you serve. It provides a framework for evaluating your performance and ensuring that your activities align with the overarching objectives of your engagement efforts. A well-crafted role statement not only guides your daily activities but also helps in communicating your role and contributions to other stakeholders, ensuring clarity and transparency in your community engagement practices.

The Mission Statement

The mission statement is a broader declaration of purpose that defines the overarching goals and values driving your work as a community engagement practitioner. It reflects your commitment to the community and outlines the fundamental principles guiding your actions and decisions.

Developing a mission statement requires introspection and a clear understanding of your values and goals. Consider what motivates you in your role and what you aim to achieve through your engagement efforts. A mission statement should be concise yet comprehensive, capturing the essence of your purpose. For example, a mission statement might read, "To empower and engage diverse community members through inclusive dialogue and collaborative initiatives, fostering sustainable development and social equity."

Your mission statement serves as a compass, directing your efforts and ensuring that your activities are aligned with your core values and objectives. It also acts as a motivational tool, reinforcing your commitment and providing a sense of direction as you navigate the complexities of community engagement.

Circle of Concern and Circle of Influence

Understanding the concepts of the circle of concern and circle of influence is crucial for effective community engagement and for strategically focusing your efforts. The circle of concern encompasses all the issues, challenges, and factors that you care about or that impact the community. This circle includes both internal and external factors that you might be worried about or interested in, ranging from local issues to broader societal trends.

In contrast, the circle of influence refers to the areas where you have the capacity to effect change or make an impact. It is the subset of the circle of concern where your actions can directly influence outcomes. Recognizing the distinction between these two circles helps you focus your efforts on areas where you can make a meaningful difference, rather than expending energy on concerns beyond your control.

To effectively perform your role, it is essential to identify and prioritize the elements within your circle of influence. This involves assessing your strengths, resources, and opportunities for impact. By concentrating on areas where you can exercise influence, you can develop targeted strategies and interventions that align with your role statement and mission statement.

For example, if a significant concern in your community is the lack of access to educational resources, your circle of influence might involve organizing community workshops, partnering with local educational institutions, and advocating for additional resources. While you may be concerned about broader systemic issues, focusing on actionable steps within your circle of influence enables you to create tangible and impactful outcomes.

Integration and Application

Integrating your role statement, mission statement, and understanding of the circles of concern and influence involves aligning your daily activities and strategic planning with your broader goals. Start by ensuring that your role statement clearly supports your mission statement and that your actions are directed toward achieving the objectives outlined in your mission.

Regularly reflect on your circle of concern and circle of influence to adjust your strategies and focus. By maintaining a clear understanding of these concepts, you can effectively manage your resources and efforts, ensuring that you are making a meaningful impact within your capacity.

In conclusion, crafting a well-defined role statement and mission statement, coupled with a strategic understanding of the circle of concern and circle of influence, is vital for effective community engagement. These elements guide your actions, align your efforts with broader goals, and help you focus on areas where you can achieve significant impact. By integrating these principles into your practice, you enhance your ability to contribute meaningfully to community development and foster positive change.

5.5. Summary

Chapter 5 offers a comprehensive exploration of frameworks and principles essential for effective community engagement and development. It emphasizes the importance of integrating robust frameworks such as Participatory Action Research (PAR) and participative democracy to enhance community involvement and impact.

PAR is introduced as a collaborative research methodology that merges research and action to address local issues through collective inquiry. Its core principles—collaboration, reflection, and iterative learning—are vital for ensuring that research is both relevant and actionable. PAR fosters a participatory approach where community members actively contribute to every stage of the research process, from problem identification to solution implementation.

This approach not only empowers communities but also ensures that research outcomes directly address local needs.

The chapter further elaborates on building a strong evidence base for community engagement, stressing the need to go beyond traditional quantitative evaluations. Drawing from Auspos and Kubisch (2004[76]), it highlights the value of incorporating qualitative data and contextual information to capture the full spectrum of community dynamics. By using qualitative methods like interviews and focus groups, practitioners can gain deeper insights into the lived experiences of community members and the broader socio-economic context. This comprehensive approach allows for a better understanding of the root causes of community issues and the long-term effects of interventions.

The concept of participative democracy is explored as a complement to representative democracy. While representative democracy involves decision-making by elected officials, participative democracy requires direct community involvement in governance processes. This approach ensures that policies and initiatives reflect the actual needs and aspirations of the community, fostering greater accountability and transparency. The chapter also discusses the challenges faced by larger agencies in maintaining meaningful engagement and suggests strategies such as decentralizing decision-making and leveraging technology to enhance participative processes.

A practice framework for integrative partnerships is detailed, emphasizing the iterative nature of PAR. It outlines a structured process starting from defining the initial question and designing

---

76 Auspos P, Kubisch A (2004) Building knowledge about community change – moving beyond evaluations. Washington: The Aspen institute Roundtable on Community Change.

research collaboratively with the community, to refining the research focus based on real-time insights and validating findings with community members. This iterative approach ensures that research and interventions remain responsive to the community's evolving needs.

The chapter also addresses the principles of Action Research and Action Learning, which advocate for flexible, responsive project development rather than adhering to pre-determined outcomes. These frameworks emphasize ongoing community engagement, iterative planning, and continuous reflection, allowing projects to adapt to new insights and changing conditions. Ensuring transparency and building accountability through regular communication and documentation of lessons learned are key to maintaining trust and effectiveness in community projects.

Finally, the chapter underscores the importance of clearly defining the role of community engagement practitioners through a role statement and mission statement. It also discusses the concepts of the circle of concern and circle of influence, advising practitioners to focus their efforts on areas where they can make a meaningful impact. By aligning their actions with these principles, practitioners can enhance their effectiveness, contribute to sustainable community development, and foster positive change.

In summary, Chapter 5 provides a comprehensive overview of frameworks and methodologies crucial for effective community engagement. By integrating participatory approaches, building a robust evidence base, and employing flexible project frameworks, practitioners can develop initiatives that are both impactful and responsive to community needs.

CHAPTER 6
GOVERNMENT AND COMMUNITY PARTNERSHIPS

6.1. Introduction

This chapter explores the Australian Government structured across three levels: Commonwealth, state, and local governments. The Commonwealth handles national matters like defense and foreign policy, impacting all states and territories. State governments manage regional issues such as health and education, with significant variation based on population and geography. Local governments focus on community-specific tasks like urban planning and waste management, with responsibilities ranging from small rural areas to large metropolitan regions. Effective community engagement requires navigating the overlaps and interactions between these levels, ensuring cohesive and responsive initiatives that address diverse local needs and challenges.

- Evaluating roles that comes under the banner of 'Government' including, elected representatives, policy makers, managers and practitioners.

- Community Services development - is influenced by the interplay between Commonwealth, state, and local governments. The Commonwealth sets national priorities and provides broad funding, while state governments implement regional policies and programs tailored to specific needs. Local governments focus on community-level services, addressing immediate needs like public amenities and local support. Effective community service development relies on coordinating these efforts across all government levels to ensure that services are comprehensive, responsive, and aligned with local needs and priorities.
- Community engagement and government functions
- Facilitate, advocate and regulate
- Working with spirit

6.1. Australian Government structure

In Australia, the landscape of governance is shaped by three distinct spheres of government: the Commonwealth, state, and local governments. Each of these spheres plays a crucial role in the functioning of the country, with their responsibilities and areas of focus varying widely. Understanding the interplay between these levels of government and their interactions with community organizations is essential for effective community engagement and development.

The Commonwealth government, also known as the federal government, operates at the national level and is responsible for approximately 20 million Australians. Its responsibilities span a broad range of areas including national defense, immigration, foreign policy, and large-scale economic management. The Commonwealth's policies and programs often have far-reaching impacts across the entire country, and its decisions can influence both state and local governments. Given its extensive jurisdiction and significant budgetary capacity, the Commonwealth plays a pivotal role in setting national priorities and providing funding for various projects and initiatives.

In contrast, state governments manage affairs within their respective states or territories, overseeing areas such as health, education, transport, and law enforcement. With each state having its own government, there is a considerable degree of variation in how these responsibilities are executed. States like New South Wales and Victoria have large populations and extensive geographic areas, while others, such as Tasmania or the Northern Territory, cover smaller populations but vast and often remote regions. This variation influences how state governments interact with local communities and shape local policies and services.

Local governments, the third tier in Australia's federal system, operate at the community level. Their responsibilities are highly localized, ranging from urban planning and waste management to community services and local road maintenance. The scope of local government functions can vary greatly depending on the size and demographic characteristics of the area. In Western Australia, for instance, local councils might oversee a community as small as 250 people in rural areas, while metropolitan councils in major cities like Perth or Sydney could manage populations exceeding 100,000. This discrepancy in scale reflects the diverse needs and challenges faced by local governments across different regions.

The overlapping responsibilities among these three levels of government can sometimes create complexities in policy implementation and community engagement. For instance, a local council might work in tandem with state and federal agencies on a development project, requiring coordination across multiple jurisdictions. Each level of government may have its own set of priorities, regulations, and funding mechanisms, which can affect how community needs are addressed and resources are allocated.

Moreover, the geographic focus of each sphere of government plays a significant role in shaping their interactions with communities. The Commonwealth's national perspective often means that its policies need to be adaptable to the varied conditions of different states and territories. In contrast, state governments must tailor their approaches to the specific needs of their regions, while local governments are directly engaged with the daily lives of residents and are often the most attuned to local issues and concerns.

Effective community partnerships hinge on understanding these differences and navigating the interactions between government levels. Collaboration among the Commonwealth, state, and local governments can lead to more cohesive and impactful community initiatives. By aligning objectives and coordinating efforts, these partnerships can address complex issues that span multiple jurisdictions, ensuring that community needs are met comprehensively and efficiently.

In summary, Australia's three spheres of government each play a unique and essential role in the governance landscape. The Commonwealth oversees national issues with a broad perspective, state governments handle regional matters with varying focus, and local governments address the immediate needs of individual communities. Understanding these roles and their intersections is crucial for fostering effective government-community partnerships and ensuring that community engagement efforts are both strategic and responsive to local needs.

6.2. Government roles and modes of state response to community participation

In examining the roles within the sphere of 'Government' in community development, it is essential to understand the distinct functions of elected representatives, policy makers, managers, and practitioners, as well as the varying modes of state response to community participation. Research by Hancock (1999) and Midgley et al. (1986) provides valuable insights into these dynamics.

Elected representatives, including members of parliament and local councilors, serve as the voice of their constituents, bringing community issues and needs to the legislative arena. Their role is to advocate for policies and allocate resources that reflect the priorities of the people they represent. Policy makers, on the other hand, are tasked with crafting and shaping policies based on research, expert advice, and strategic goals. They work within a framework of political and social considerations to develop policies that aim to address broad societal issues.

Managers in government agencies implement policies and oversee the delivery of services, ensuring that programs are carried out effectively and efficiently. They coordinate between different departments and levels of government, and their role is crucial in translating policy into tangible outcomes. Practitioners, including social workers, community organizers, and service providers, operate on the ground, directly engaging with communities to deliver services and support. Their work is pivotal in addressing immediate needs and fostering local development.

Hancock's (1999[77]) analysis highlights four distinct modes of

---

[77] Hancock, T. (2009). Act Locally: Community-based population health promotion. Ottawa: Senate Sub-Committee on Population Health, Government of Canada.

state response to community participation: the anti-participatory mode, the manipulative mode, the incremental mode, and the participatory mode. The anti-participatory mode reflects a state stance that actively discourages or ignores community input, often leading to disengagement and dissatisfaction among community members. In the manipulative mode, the state superficially engages with communities but does not genuinely empower them, instead using participation as a tool for achieving pre-determined outcomes.

The incremental mode represents a more moderate approach, where the state allows for some degree of community involvement but within a controlled framework that limits the scope of influence. This approach can lead to gradual improvements but may fall short of fostering deep, meaningful participation. In contrast, the participatory mode embodies a genuine commitment to engaging communities in decision-making processes. This approach values and incorporates community input into policy development and service delivery, recognizing the benefits of collaborative engagement in achieving more effective and responsive outcomes.

Understanding these roles and modes of response is crucial for community development practitioners, as it informs how they navigate interactions with government entities and advocate for meaningful community involvement. By recognizing the complexities of these relationships and the varying degrees of state engagement, practitioners can better strategize their efforts to promote genuine, effective community participation and development.

6.3. Community service development perspective.

In the realm of community service development, establishing effective partnerships between government and community organizations is crucial. These partnerships hinge on several key elements: planning, funding and accountability, policy development, and resourcing, all of which play pivotal roles in shaping successful community outcomes.

Planning is the first and perhaps the most critical stage in any community service development initiative. It involves a collaborative process where government agencies and community organizations come together to identify community needs, set objectives, and design strategies to address those needs. This stage requires a thorough understanding of local issues, available resources, and the capacities of all stakeholders involved. Effective planning ensures that initiatives are well-coordinated, targeted, and aligned with the needs of the community, leading to more sustainable and impactful outcomes.

Funding and accountability are integral aspects of implementing community service projects. Governments often provide financial resources to support community programs, but this funding comes with expectations of transparency and accountability. Partnerships must ensure that funds are used effectively and efficiently, adhering to agreed-upon budgets and reporting requirements. This involves establishing clear mechanisms for financial oversight, regular monitoring, and evaluation of spending. Accountability measures help maintain trust between government bodies and community organizations, ensuring that resources are directed towards achieving the intended goals.

Figure 8 - Community service development (CSD)

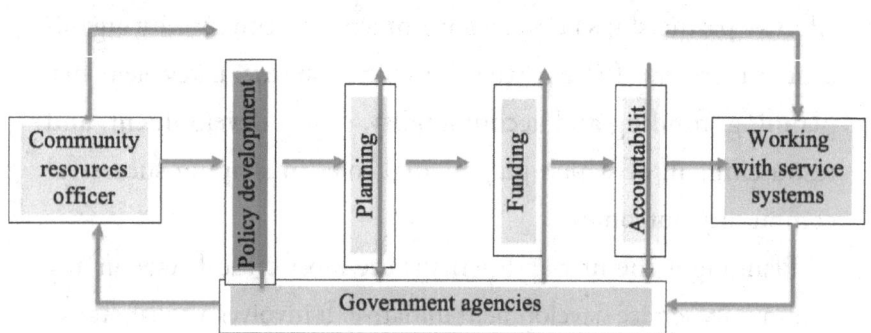

Policy development is another critical component of government-community partnerships. Effective policies are developed through a process of consultation and collaboration, incorporating input from community members and organizations. This collaborative approach helps ensure that policies are responsive to local needs and are designed with practical implementation in mind. Policymakers must work closely with community practitioners to understand the on-the-ground realities and incorporate their insights into policy frameworks. This not only enhances the relevance of policies but also fosters a sense of ownership and commitment among community stakeholders.

Resourcing, which encompasses both financial and non-financial support, is essential for the successful execution of community service initiatives. Beyond funding, resources include access to expertise, facilities, and networks that can amplify the impact of community programs. Governments can support community organizations by providing technical assistance, training, and access to resources that enable them to deliver services more effectively. Building strong partnerships means not only committing financial resources but also fostering a collaborative environment where both parties share knowledge, skills, and resources.

Overall, the success of government and community partnerships in service development depends on a well-orchestrated approach that integrates planning, funding and accountability, policy development, and resourcing. By engaging in thoughtful and collaborative planning, ensuring transparent and accountable use of funds, developing responsive policies, and providing adequate resources, these partnerships can address community needs more effectively and build stronger, more resilient communities.

6.4. Community engagement – Responsive government policy and practice

Engaging communities in the development of responsive government policy and practice is an essential aspect of effective governance. This process is not merely about informing communities of decisions but actively involving them in shaping policies that affect their lives. As highlighted by Cavaye in 2005, a significant challenge is the perception that "governments are not listening." This perception underscores the need for a more inclusive and participatory approach to policy development.

To address this issue, it is crucial for governments to move beyond tokenistic engagement and genuinely incorporate community input into the decision-making process. This involves creating spaces where community voices are not only heard but also valued and acted upon. Genuine engagement requires building trust between government officials and community members. It starts with recognizing the diverse perspectives within a community and

Figure 9 - Analysing engagement process

Inform	Consult	Involve	Collaborate	Empower
to inform or educate stakeholders in one-way communication, there is no invitation to respond	to gain information and feedback from stakeholders to inform decisions made internally. Limited two-way communication - ask questions, stakeholder provides answers	to work directly with stakeholders throughout the process to ensure that issues and concerns are understood and considered. Two-way or multi-way communication where learning takes place on both sides	to partner with stakeholder and/or stakeholder groups for the development of mutually agreed solutions and joint plan of action. Two-way/multi-way communication where learning, negotiation and decision making on both sides. Stakeholders work together to take action	to delegate decision-making in the hands of the stakeholders on a particular issue. Stakeholders are enabled/equipped to actively contribute to the achievement of outcomes
We will keep you informed	We will keep you informed, listen to your concerns, consider your insights, and provide feedback on our decisions	We will work with you so that your concerns and issues are directly reflected in alternatives developed and provide feedback on how input influenced the outcome	We will work together to agree on what we will implement and incorporate your advice and recommendations into the outcomes to the maximum extent possible	We will implement what you decide and we will support and complement your actions

ensuring that engagement processes are accessible to all, particularly marginalized and underrepresented groups.

Effective community engagement begins with establishing clear and open channels of communication. Governments must proactively seek out community feedback through various methods such as public consultations, surveys, and community forums. It is essential that these methods are designed to reach a broad audience and encourage diverse participation. This may involve utilizing multiple communication platforms, including digital and traditional media, to engage different segments of the community.

Moreover, it is important to foster a culture of transparency and responsiveness. Governments should not only solicit input but also demonstrate how this input is influencing policy decisions. Feedback loops that show how community suggestions are incorporated into policy development can enhance trust and encourage continued engagement. When communities see that their contributions have a tangible impact, they are more likely to participate actively in future engagements.

Integrating community perspectives into policy development also requires a commitment to capacity building. Governments should invest in resources and training to help community members effectively engage in the policy process. This might include providing workshops on policy issues, offering support for community-led research, or developing tools that empower individuals to voice their concerns and ideas.

Furthermore, it is crucial to recognize that community engagement is an ongoing process, not a one-time event. Building lasting relationships with community members requires continuous dialogue and iterative feedback. Governments should establish regular engagement practices that allow for ongoing consultation and adaptation of policies based on evolving community needs.

In conclusion, to overcome the challenge of governments not listening as noted by Cavaye, a shift towards deeper, more meaningful community engagement is essential. By creating inclusive processes, fostering transparency, and continuously building relationships with community members, governments can develop more responsive and effective policies. This approach not only enhances policy outcomes but also strengthens the trust and collaboration between governments and the communities they serve.

6.5. Summary

This chapter delves into the intricate structure of the Australian government, which operates through three distinct levels: Commonwealth, state, and local governments. Each level plays a unique and crucial role in the governance landscape, with their responsibilities and interactions shaping the delivery of public services and community engagement.

The Commonwealth government, operating at the national level, is responsible for broad, overarching issues such as national defence, foreign policy, and immigration, affecting all states and territories. Its policies and funding decisions have far-reaching impacts, setting national priorities and influencing state and local governments. With its vast budget and jurisdiction, the Commonwealth plays a pivotal role in establishing frameworks and providing resources for various national initiatives.

In contrast, state governments manage more localized affairs within their jurisdictions. They handle critical areas like health, education, transport, and law enforcement, tailoring policies to address regional needs. States vary significantly in terms of population and geographic scope. For instance, New South Wales and Victoria have large, densely populated areas, while Tasmania and the Northern Territory have smaller populations but more remote and expansive regions. This variation affects how state governments interact with local communities and shape regional policies.

Local governments, the third tier of Australia's federal system, are directly engaged with community-level issues. They oversee functions such as urban planning, waste management, and local road maintenance. The scale of local government responsibilities can differ greatly, from small rural councils with a few hundred residents to large metropolitan councils managing populations exceeding 100,000. This disparity highlights the diverse needs and challenges faced by local governments.

Navigating the overlaps between these levels of government can be complex. For example, a local council may collaborate with state and federal agencies on development projects, requiring coordination across various jurisdictions. Each government tier has its priorities, regulations, and funding mechanisms, which can influence how resources are allocated and community needs are addressed.

Effective community engagement and service development depend on understanding and managing these interactions. The Commonwealth sets national priorities and provides broad funding, while state governments implement policies and programs tailored to regional needs. Local governments address immediate community concerns and manage local services. Coordinating these efforts is crucial for ensuring that services are comprehensive, responsive, and aligned with local needs.

The chapter also explores the roles within the government, including elected representatives, policy makers, managers, and practitioners, and how these roles influence community participation. Elected representatives advocate for community needs at the legislative level, while policy makers develop policies based on expert advice and strategic goals. Managers oversee policy implementation and service delivery, and practitioners work directly with communities to provide services and support. Hancock (1999) and Midgley et al. (1986) provide insights into the modes of state response to community participation, from anti-participatory to genuinely participatory approaches. Understanding these dynamics helps practitioners navigate government interactions and advocate for meaningful community involvement.

Finally, the chapter addresses the importance of engaging communities in policy development, referencing Cavaye's (2005[78]) observation that governments are often perceived as not listening. To overcome this, governments must move beyond superficial engagement and incorporate community input genuinely. This involves establishing transparent communication channels, fostering trust, and demonstrating how community feedback influences policy decisions. Ongoing dialogue and capacity building are essential for effective community engagement, ensuring that policies are responsive and reflective of community needs.

In summary, the chapter underscores the need for a coordinated approach among the Commonwealth, state, and local governments to address community needs effectively. By understanding their roles and interactions, fostering genuine engagement, and ensuring transparent and responsive practices, governments can build stronger, more effective partnerships with the communities they serve.

---

[78] Cavaye, J., & Ross, H. (2022). Community resilience and community development: What mutual opportunities arise from interactions between the two concepts?. Community Development for Times of Crisis, 75-96.

PART THREE

SKILLS IN WORKING WITH COMMUNITIES: CALD (CULTURALLY AND LINGUISTICALLY DIVERSE) PERSPECTIVE

This chapter delves into the essential soft skills and emotional intelligence required for effective community engagement. It emphasizes the importance of negotiating and agreeing on shared values within communities, which is crucial for fostering collaboration and understanding. The skills discussed are universally applicable across various disciplines, making them valuable not only to practitioners but also to community members.

Chapter 7 explores community decision-making, focusing on how to address national interests and cultural issues while promoting integration over segregation. It examines the role of diasporic interventions in shaping inclusive decision-making processes.

Chapter 8 addresses community partnerships, highlighting

strategies for building effective collaborations with diverse ethical and cultural groups. It underscores the importance of mutual respect and understanding in enhancing partnership outcomes.

Chapter 9 focuses on effective community planning, with a strong emphasis on social justice and human rights. It details techniques for community profiling and planning that ensure equity and responsiveness to community needs.

Chapter 10, "Leading with Spirit – Leadership, Energy, and Empowerment," discusses the long-term commitment required for successful community work. It stresses that short-term engagement is insufficient for meaningful impact. Practitioners and community members need to be adaptable and proactive, with well-developed strategies and contingency plans to address societal changes and maximize positive outcomes for the community. The chapter also touches on the importance of balancing development pace with practical application, theory, and practice to achieve sustainable progress.

CHAPTER 7
COMMUNITY DECISION MAKING

Introduction

This chapter will:

- Aim to address the complexities and opportunities inherent in participative decision-making, particularly within culturally and linguistically diverse (CaLD) communities. It provides a comprehensive examination of the challenges associated with involving diverse groups in decision-making processes and offers practical strategies for fostering meaningful engagement.

The chapter begins by exploring the challenges faced in participative decision-making. Engaging CaLD communities can be fraught with difficulties, including language barriers, cultural differences, and varying levels of familiarity with democratic processes. These challenges can hinder effective participation and result in decisions that do not fully reflect the needs or preferences of these communities. Understanding these obstacles is crucial for developing strategies that promote inclusivity and ensure that all voices are heard and valued.

An essential component of the chapter is the examination of hierarchy and organizational structures in decision-making. The chapter outlines how traditional hierarchical models of decision-making can sometimes exclude CaLD community members from meaningful participation. It discusses the importance of flattening organizational structures to create more inclusive environments where community input is genuinely integrated into the decision-making process. This includes revising structures to facilitate greater collaboration and ensure that decision-making bodies are representative of the community's diversity.

key principles for decision-making within CaLD communities, focusing on respect, equity, and cultural sensitivity. It emphasizes the need for decision-makers to approach these communities with a commitment to understanding and addressing cultural nuances. This involves recognizing the unique values and perspectives of different cultural groups and ensuring that decision-making processes are adaptable to these diverse needs. Principles such as transparency, inclusivity, and responsiveness are highlighted as fundamental to fostering trust and effective participation.

To facilitate better involvement of CaLD members in decision-making, the chapter proposes several techniques. These include employing culturally competent facilitators who can bridge gaps between decision-makers and community members, utilizing multilingual resources to ensure effective communication, and creating safe spaces for open dialogue. It also recommends using participatory methods such as focus groups, community forums, and surveys that are tailored to the specific needs and preferences of

CaLD groups. By implementing these techniques, organizations can enhance engagement and ensure that decision-making processes are truly inclusive.

Finally, the chapter addresses the importance of responsibility and community ownership in the decision-making process. It underscores that for participative decision-making to be successful, community members must feel a sense of ownership over the outcomes. This involves not only involving them in the decision-making process but also empowering them to take an active role in implementing and evaluating decisions. Encouraging community ownership fosters a deeper commitment to shared goals and enhances the sustainability of initiatives.

In summary, this chapter provides a detailed exploration of the goals and strategies for improving participative decision-making in CaLD communities. By addressing challenges, restructuring decision-making processes, adhering to key principles, employing effective techniques, and fostering responsibility and ownership, practitioners can create more inclusive and equitable decision-making environments that truly reflect the diversity and needs of these communities.

7.1. Introduction

Community decision-making is a cornerstone of effective community development, as it empowers individuals to shape how programs and services are delivered. At its heart, community decision-making is about giving people a voice and ensuring that their diverse perspectives inform the outcomes that affect their lives. However, facilitating a decision-making process that is genuinely collaborative, inclusive, and effective presents significant challenges.

One of the central difficulties lies in accommodating the varied perspectives of community members. People come to the table with different values, attitudes, and priorities shaped by their unique backgrounds and experiences. This diversity, while enriching, can also complicate the decision-making process. For instance, what one group values highly might be of less concern to another, and reconciling these differences into a cohesive approach can be daunting.

Furthermore, the decision-making process often operates within tight time frames. This urgency can exacerbate challenges, as the pressure to reach a consensus quickly may lead to oversimplifications or the exclusion of minority viewpoints. Balancing the need for expedient decisions with the imperative of thorough and inclusive deliberation requires a nuanced approach.

Facilitators and community members alike grapple with these issues. A practitioner's role is to guide the process in a way that respects and integrates the range of perspectives while striving to reach decisions that are equitable and practical. This involves employing various strategies to ensure that all voices are heard. For example, creating structured opportunities for input, such as workshops or focus groups, can help ensure that diverse opinions are considered. However, these methods must be carefully designed to be accessible and welcoming to all community members.

Moreover, effective decision-making requires a commitment to transparency and open communication. Ensuring that the process is transparent helps build trust and encourages broader participation. Community members are more likely to engage meaningfully when they understand how their input will be used and when they see that their contributions are valued.

Negotiating the integration of diverse views into the final

decision can be challenging. It requires not only good facilitation skills but also the ability to navigate conflicts and find common ground. Practitioners must be adept at mediating disagreements and fostering an environment where compromise is possible. This often involves making tough choices and prioritizing certain needs or perspectives over others, which can be a source of tension.

Ultimately, successful community decision-making is an iterative process. It involves ongoing dialogue, feedback, and adjustments to ensure that the decisions made continue to reflect the community's evolving needs and priorities. It's a dynamic process that requires flexibility, patience, and a deep commitment to inclusivity.

In a nutshell, while community decision-making is essential for ensuring that programs and services meet the needs of those they are intended to serve, it is also fraught with challenges. Practitioners must navigate a landscape of diverse perspectives, tight deadlines, and complex negotiations to create decision-making processes that are both collaborative and effective. Despite these challenges, the goal remains to empower communities and ensure that their voices shape the decisions that impact their lives.

7.2. Challenges of participative decision making

The emphasis on participative decision-making in community development is central to fostering inclusive and effective programs and services. This process involves various stakeholders—communities, practitioners, consultants, and government agencies—each bringing distinct perspectives, priorities, and power bases to the table. Understanding and managing these different agendas and power dynamics is essential for creating decisions that are both relevant and effective.

As Warren (1970[79]) and Stone (1992[80]) have noted, the participative decision-making process is inherently complex due to the diverse interests and influence of different groups. Communities themselves are rich with diverse skills, knowledge, and experience. Residents possess intimate insights into their local environment, social dynamics, and the practical realities of how their community functions. This grassroots knowledge is crucial, as it provides a grounded understanding of community needs and preferences.

In contrast, practitioners, consultants, professionals, and government agencies contribute specialized knowledge from their respective disciplines. Practitioners offer insights into best practices and methodologies for community engagement and program implementation. Consultants bring expertise in areas such as strategic planning, evaluation, and policy analysis. Professionals in fields like social work, public health, and urban planning provide valuable information about specific social and health issues, while government agencies supply resources, funding, and broader regulatory frameworks.

The crux of participative decision-making lies in integrating these varied sources of knowledge to formulate programs and services that are not only technically sound but also practically relevant and accessible to the community. The challenge is to blend community insights with professional expertise while adhering to program guidelines and ensuring that all voices are heard.

One key aspect of this process is managing the power dynamics inherent in decision-making. Different stakeholders hold varying

---

[79] Warren, M. R. (2009). Community Organizing in Britain: The Political Engagement of Faith–Based Social Capital. City & Community, 8(2), 99-127.

[80] Stone, C. N. (2000). Civic engagement in American democracy.

degrees of influence based on their roles and resources. For instance, government agencies and funders often wield significant power due to their control over financial resources and policy authority. Meanwhile, community members may have less formal power but possess crucial experiential knowledge that can greatly influence the effectiveness of programs.

Balancing these power dynamics involves creating a decision-making environment where each group's contributions are valued and considered. Effective facilitators must navigate these dynamics by ensuring that community voices are not overshadowed by the more dominant interests of professionals or agencies. This might involve employing techniques such as structured dialogue sessions, feedback loops, and consensus-building exercises to ensure that the community's perspectives are genuinely incorporated into the decision-making process.

Another critical challenge is maintaining alignment between community knowledge and program guidelines. While it is essential to respect and integrate community insights, practitioners and consultants must also ensure that the resulting programs adhere to established standards and regulations. This requires a delicate balance of creativity and compliance, where community input is woven into the fabric of program design without compromising necessary guidelines and best practices.

The integration of diverse knowledge sources into a coherent decision-making process can lead to more effective and responsive programs. When community members feel that their input has shaped the outcomes, they are more likely to engage with and support the programs, resulting in better implementation and sustainability.

Participative decision-making in community development involves a complex interplay of diverse agendas, power bases, and knowledge sources. Balancing these elements requires skillful facilitation and a commitment to integrating community insights with professional expertise. By navigating these challenges, practitioners and stakeholders can create programs and services that are both relevant and accessible, ultimately leading to more effective and inclusive community outcomes.

7.3. Hierarchy and Organizational structure for decision making
In the realm of community development, understanding the hierarchy and organizational structure for decision-making is crucial for fostering effective collaboration and achieving meaningful outcomes. The organizational structure dictates how decisions are made, who is involved, and how power and responsibilities are distributed among stakeholders. This structure can significantly impact the efficacy of community programs and initiatives.

Imagine a community development project aimed at improving local public spaces. The decision-making process for such a project typically involves multiple layers of hierarchy and organizational roles, each contributing to the overall process.

At the top of this hierarchy often sits the governing body or steering committee, which may include representatives from government agencies, funding bodies, and key community leaders. This group holds the authority to make high-level decisions, such as approving budgets, setting project priorities, and establishing overall objectives. Their role is to provide strategic direction and ensure that the project aligns with broader policy goals and resource availability. For instance, in a project to revamp a neighborhood park, this group

Figure 10 - Smart Organization

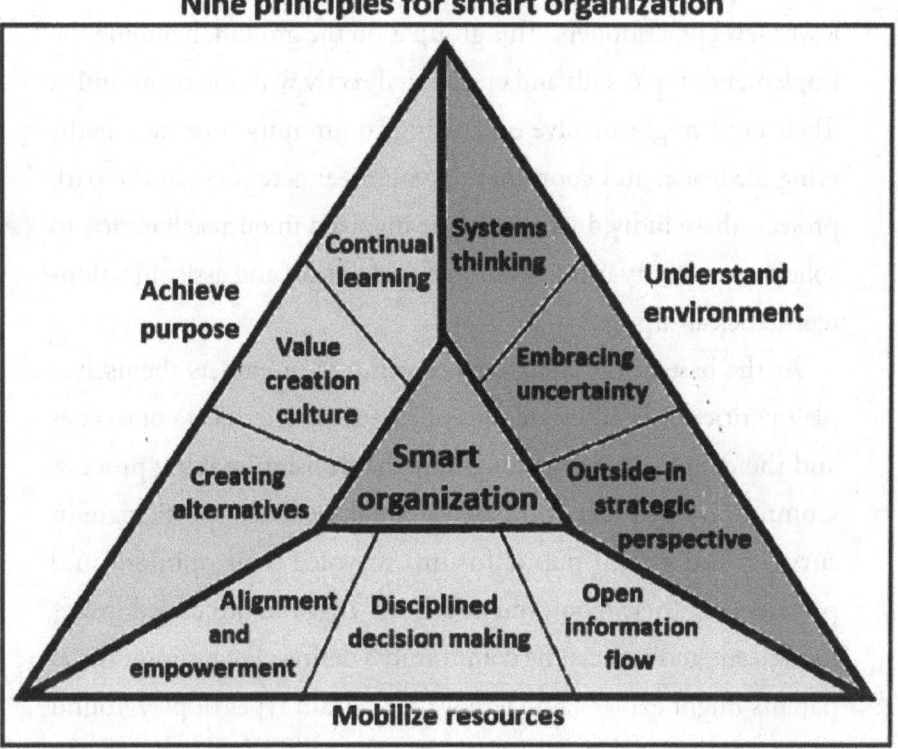

would decide on the project's scope, such as whether to include new playground equipment or enhance landscaping.

Beneath the steering committee is typically a project management team or executive committee. This group is responsible for translating strategic directives into actionable plans. It includes project managers, senior practitioners, and consultants who develop detailed project plans, timelines, and resource allocations. Their role is to ensure that the project's vision is implemented effectively and that day-to-day operations are managed smoothly. For the park renovation, this team would oversee the selection of contractors, coordinate with designers, and manage the construction process.

Further down the hierarchy, the operational team or working group consists of community members, local volunteers, and lower-level practitioners. This group is on the ground, handling the implementation details and engaging directly with the community. Their tasks might involve organizing community meetings, gathering feedback, and coordinating volunteer activities. In the park project, these individuals would be involved in outreach efforts to solicit community input on design preferences and assist in volunteer-led clean-up events.

At the base of the hierarchy, community members themselves play a critical role. They are the end-users of the project's outcomes and their input is vital throughout the decision-making process. Community members provide essential feedback, participate in surveys, and attend public forums to voice their opinions and preferences. Their involvement ensures that the project addresses local needs and reflects the community's desires. For example, local parents might express a preference for certain types of playground equipment or safety features based on their experiences and needs.

This hierarchical structure illustrates how different levels of decision-making interact to shape community projects. The steering committee provides overarching guidance and resources, the project management team executes the strategy, the operational team implements the plans, and the community provides critical feedback and engagement. Each level has distinct responsibilities and authority, yet they must work cohesively to ensure that decisions are made effectively and reflect the needs of the community.

Furthermore, understanding this structure is essential for navigating potential challenges. Conflicts may arise if there is a lack of alignment between the strategic goals set by the steering committee

Figure 11 - Structure and decision making models

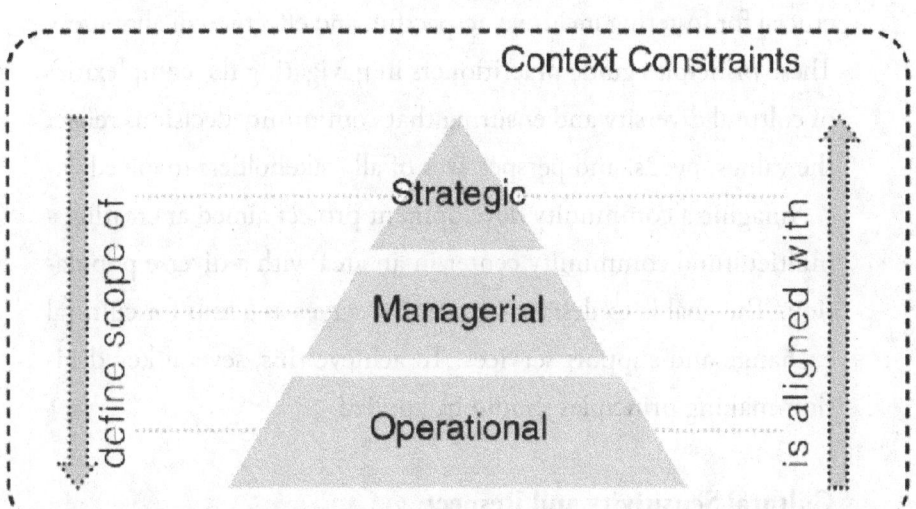

and the practical needs identified by the community. Effective communication and coordination between different levels of the hierarchy are crucial for resolving such conflicts and ensuring that the project remains on track.

The hierarchy and organizational structure for decision-making in community development are foundational to achieving successful outcomes. Each level of the hierarchy—ranging from governing bodies to community members—plays a distinct yet interconnected role in shaping and implementing community initiatives. By recognizing and leveraging these roles effectively, practitioners can enhance collaboration, address diverse needs, and ultimately create more impactful and sustainable community programs.

7.4. Key decision-making principles in CaLD communities

In community development, particularly when engaging with Culturally and Linguistically Diverse (CaLD) communities, understanding and applying key decision-making principles is crucial for fostering inclusive, respectful, and effective collaboration. These principles guide practitioners in navigating the complexities of cultural diversity and ensuring that community decisions reflect the values, needs, and perspectives of all stakeholders involved.

Imagine a community development project aimed at creating a multicultural community center in an area with a diverse population. The goal is to design a space that serves as a hub for cultural exchange and support services. To achieve this, several key decision-making principles should be applied.

Cultural Sensitivity and Respect
The first principle is cultural sensitivity and respect. This involves recognizing and valuing the diverse cultural backgrounds of community members. For instance, in designing the community centre, it's essential to consider the cultural practices, traditions, and preferences of the various groups within the CaLD community. This might include incorporating elements that reflect different cultural heritages, such as art or design motifs that resonate with various traditions, or providing multilingual signage and resources to accommodate different language needs. By demonstrating cultural sensitivity, practitioners can ensure that the community centre feels welcoming and inclusive to all members.

Participatory Approach
The second principle is a participatory approach. Engaging community members in the decision-making process is vital for ensuring that their voices are heard and their needs are met. For the community centre project, this means organizing focus groups, surveys,

and public meetings where members of the CaLD community can provide input on the design and functions of the centre. For example, organizing a series of workshops where different cultural groups can discuss what services and features they would like to see can lead to a more inclusive design. This participatory approach not only enhances the relevance of the project but also fosters a sense of ownership and commitment among community members.

Equity and Inclusivity
Equity and inclusivity are key principles in decision-making for CaLD communities. This involves addressing power imbalances and ensuring that all community members, especially those from marginalized or less represented groups, have an equal opportunity to participate and influence decisions. In the context of the community centre, this might involve ensuring that resources are allocated fairly, so that no particular group feels excluded or underrepresented. For instance, if some groups have fewer resources or less access to decision-making forums, practitioners might provide additional support or tailored outreach efforts to ensure their voices are included.

Transparency and Accountability
Transparency and accountability are crucial for building trust and ensuring that decisions are made fairly. This means clearly communicating the decision-making process, criteria, and outcomes to the community. In the case of the community center, practitioners should provide regular updates on the project's progress, how community feedback is being incorporated, and how decisions are being made. This could involve creating a project website

or newsletter where stakeholders can track developments and see how their input has influenced the project. Transparency helps to manage expectations and build trust between practitioners and the community.

Cultural Competence

Cultural competence is the principle of understanding and effectively interacting with people from diverse cultural backgrounds. Practitioners should be aware of cultural norms and practices and how these might influence decision-making processes. For example, understanding different communication styles, decision-making hierarchies within various cultural groups, and preferences for group versus individual consultations can improve engagement and ensure that interactions are respectful and productive. Involving cultural liaisons or community representatives who have a deep understanding of the various cultures within the CaLD community can enhance the effectiveness of the decision-making process.

Flexibility and Adaptability

Finally, flexibility and adaptability are essential principles. The needs and priorities of CaLD communities can evolve over time, and decision-making processes should be able to adapt to these changes. Practitioners must be prepared to revise plans and strategies based on new information or shifting community dynamics. For instance, if a previously underrepresented group becomes more active or vocal, the decision-making process might need to be adjusted to accommodate their input and ensure that their emerging needs are addressed.

Applying key decision-making principles in CaLD communities

involves embracing cultural sensitivity, adopting a participatory approach, ensuring equity and inclusivity, maintaining transparency and accountability, developing cultural competence, and being flexible and adaptable. By adhering to these principles, community development practitioners can create more effective, respectful, and inclusive initiatives that truly reflect the diverse needs and values of the communities they serve.

7.5. Responsibility and community ownership

In the community responsibility and ownership context, recognizing the contextual factors that affect decision-making is paramount. According to Abelson (2001), one of the critical contextual factors to consider is the existing social structures and divisions between competing interests within a community. These structures and divisions can significantly influence how decisions are made and who gets to participate in the decision-making process.

Social structures in communities often encompass power dynamics, norms, values, traditions, and practices. These elements can sometimes perpetuate injustice and exclusion, leading to inequitable outcomes for certain groups or individuals. As a community development practitioner, it is essential to understand how these power structures operate and their impact on community participation. For instance, power imbalances can result in the marginalization of less dominant groups, affecting their ability to have a say in decisions that impact their lives.

Take, for example, a community planning project aimed at revitalizing a local park. In such a project, social structures and power dynamics might influence who is involved in the planning process and whose voices are heard. If certain groups hold more power or influence, they may dominate the discussion, potentially sidelining the needs and preferences of other community members. This could result in an outcome that benefits the more powerful groups at the expense of others.

To address these issues, practitioners must actively work to identify and challenge unjust power structures. This involves recognizing who holds power within the community and how it affects decision-making processes. Practitioners should assess whether these power dynamics contribute to inequity, exclusion, or marginalization and seek to create more inclusive and equitable processes.

Community values play a crucial role in facilitating involvement in decision-making. Abelson (2001) notes that shared community values can enhance participation and foster a sense of collective action. For example, in a rural community with a strong value placed on preserving local identity, there may be broad-based community involvement in projects that align with this value. When community members share a commitment to maintaining their local culture and traditions, they are more likely to engage in decision-making processes that reflect and uphold these values.

Similarly, Brehm et al. (2004[81]) highlight that a sense of community attachment and interest in the community's well-being often correlates with higher involvement in decision-making. When individuals feel a strong connection to their community and care about its overall health and progress, they are more likely to participate actively in decisions that affect it. This sense of attachment can drive

---

81 Brehm, J. M., Eisenhauer, B. W., & Krannich, R. S. (2004). Dimensions of community attachment and their relationship to well-being in the amenity-rich rural west. Rural Sociology, 69(3), 405-429.

individuals to contribute their time, resources, and ideas, leading to more engaged and informed decision-making.

In practical terms, this means that as a practitioner, you should foster an environment where community values are acknowledged and leveraged to promote participation. Engaging community members around shared values can enhance their involvement and commitment to decision-making processes. For instance, creating forums for dialogue where community members can discuss and align on shared goals can help build consensus and support for initiatives.

In conclusion, recognizing contextual factors such as social structures and community values is essential for effective decision-making in community development. By understanding and addressing power dynamics and leveraging shared community values, practitioners can create more inclusive, equitable, and engaging decision-making processes. This approach not only improves the quality of decisions but also strengthens the sense of community and collective action among its members.

7.6. Summary

This chapter provides an in-depth exploration of community development with a focus on participative decision-making. It examines the inherent challenges of engaging diverse community members in decision-making processes, particularly within the context of cultural and linguistic diversity (CaLD) communities. The complexities of decision-making are influenced by hierarchical and organizational structures, which can impact the effectiveness of participatory approaches.

Key principles for decision-making in CaLD communities

include recognizing and addressing the specific needs and perspectives of these groups, ensuring that decisions are inclusive and equitable. Techniques for involving CaLD members effectively range from culturally sensitive engagement methods to fostering strong community relationships.

Responsibility and community ownership are pivotal in ensuring that decision-making processes are not only inclusive but also lead to meaningful outcomes. Ultimately, the chapter underscores the importance of understanding the intricate dynamics of community engagement, promoting collaborative decision-making, and supporting community ownership to achieve successful development outcomes.

Practice tips

1. How do power networks within a community influence the process of inclusive decision-making? In exploring this question, consider the following aspects:
   - **Identification of Power Networks**: Investigate the key individuals and groups who hold influence within the community. This includes understanding their roles, relationships, and the sources of their power.
   - **Impact on Inclusivity:** Analyze how these power dynamics affect the inclusivity of decision-making processes. Determine whether the presence of certain power structures facilitates or hinders the participation of marginalized groups.
   - **Barriers to Participation:** Examine the barriers that these power networks might create for equitable participation. Assess how these barriers impact the representation of diverse voices in decision-making.

- **Strategies for Integration:** Explore strategies to integrate marginalized groups into decision-making despite existing power structures. Consider methods to balance power dynamics and enhance inclusive participation.
- **Outcomes and Effectiveness:** Evaluate the outcomes of decision-making processes in relation to inclusivity. Assess whether adjustments to power networks lead to more equitable and effective community decisions.

2. Working closely with the community members are essential to understand the community values and culture.
- In Western Australia, community organizations play a vital role in enhancing cultural engagement and fostering intercultural understanding through various initiatives and programs. These organizations, including the Indian Society of Western Australia, the Organisation of African Communities in Western Australia, and the Sri Lankan Cultural Society, each contribute uniquely to the cultural mosaic of the region. Their efforts are often supported by the Department of Communities[82] and the Office of Multicultural Interests (OMI) WA, which provides valuable resources and guidance to promote multiculturalism.

The Indian Society of Western Australia (ISWA) is instrumental in celebrating and preserving Indian culture within the state. Through events such as Diwali festivals, cultural fairs, and traditional dance performances, ISWA brings together people from

---

[82] Extracted from Department of Communities -Partnership framework - https://www.wa.gov.au/government/document-collections/partnerships-the-department-of-communities

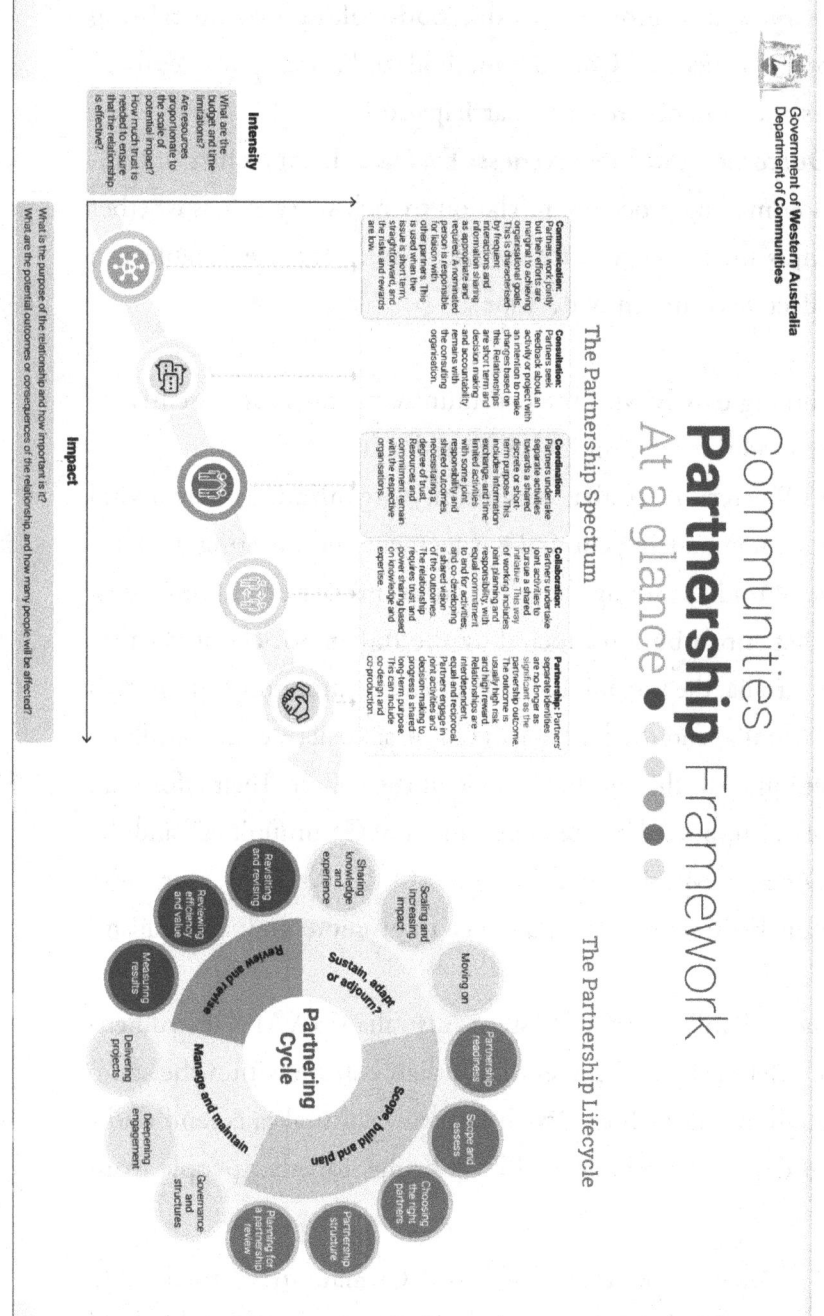

Figure 12 - Communities partnership framework

diverse backgrounds to experience the rich traditions of India. Their programs often include educational workshops on Indian cuisine, art, and language, which help to bridge cultural gaps and foster mutual respect among different communities. ISWA's activities not only cater to the Indian diaspora but also engage the wider Western Australian community, encouraging cross-cultural interaction and understanding.

The Organisation of African Communities in Western Australia (OACWA) similarly plays a crucial role in promoting African culture and heritage. Africa Day celebrations, organized by OACWA, are a prominent example of their work, offering a platform for showcasing African music, dance, and cuisine. These events are designed to highlight the diversity and unity of African cultures while addressing contemporary issues faced by African communities in Australia. By creating spaces for dialogue and cultural exchange, OACWA helps to enhance the visibility and appreciation of African heritage, contributing to a more inclusive and culturally aware society.

The Sri Lankan Cultural Society also makes significant contributions to cultural engagement in Western Australia. Through festivals such as Sinhala and Tamil New Year celebrations, cultural performances, and community gatherings, the Sri Lankan Cultural Society fosters a deeper understanding of Sri Lankan traditions and values. Their events often feature traditional music, dance, and culinary experiences that allow participants to immerse themselves in Sri Lankan culture. Additionally, the society provides support and resources for Sri Lankan immigrants, helping them to navigate their new environment while maintaining their cultural identity.

The Office of Multicultural Interests (OMI) WA plays a key role in supporting these and other community organizations.

By providing funding, guidance, and resources, OMI facilitates programs and initiatives that promote multiculturalism and social cohesion. Their support helps organizations to expand their reach and enhance their impact, ensuring that cultural engagements are inclusive and accessible to all. OMI's initiatives often include multicultural festivals, community grants, and advisory services, all of which contribute to the vibrant cultural landscape of Western Australia.

Some organisations work very actively, like the Indian Society of Western Australia, the Organisation of African Communities in Western Australia, and the Sri Lankan Cultural Society, supported by the Office of Multicultural Interests, work collaboratively to enrich cultural engagement in the region. Through their diverse programs and events, they foster intercultural understanding, celebrate cultural heritage, and strengthen community bonds, contributing to a more inclusive and harmonious society.

In Western Australia – the Indian Society of Western Australia (ISWA) [83]received a significant boost from the Mark McGowan Government, marking a transformative moment for the community organization. It can be analysed as a case study for the integration and empowerment along with combining and addressing the government criteria for securing funding and creating an impact.

---

83 Extracted from the article by Liam Ducey on Examiner newspaper – Feb 17, 2023
- https://www.yourlocalexaminer.com.au/indian-society-receives-funding-boost

Figure 13 - News article - Examiner newspaper - Feb 17, 2023

ARMADALE CANNING GOSNELLS IN THE NEWS NEWS

Indian Society receives funding boost

By **Liam Ducey** - February 17, 2023 11:59 am   2586

Indian Society of WA President Satish Nair said the Community Support Funding of $150,000 over three years would ensure the continued success of the centre.

The Indian Society of WA have received a financial boost thanks to the Office of Multicultural Interest's Community Support Fund.

The 55-year-old not-for-profit association is entirely managed by volunteers, with a 13-member management committee.

Figure 14 -Media Statement - 5 Dec 2023

06/08/2024, 08:22 McGowan Labor Government contributes $1.5 million to construct new WA Indian Community Centre | Western Australian Government

GOVERNMENT OF WESTERN AUSTRALIA

1. Home
2. WA Government
3. Media statements
4. McGowan Labor Government
5. McGowan Labor Government contributes $1.5 million to construct new WA Indian Community Centre

McGowan Labor Government contributes $1.5 million to construct new WA Indian Community Centre

The McGowan Labor Government will contribute $1.5 million to the construction of a new WA Indian Community Centre in Willetton to benefit the Indian community in Western Australia.

- New building to be constructed on site secured through a Lotterywest grant
- Indian Society of WA to lead development of the centre, with every Indian community group in WA able to use facility

The McGowan Labor Government will contribute $1.5 million to the construction of a new WA Indian Community Centre in Willetton to benefit the Indian community in Western Australia.

The Indian Society of Western Australia (ISWA), the peak body for WA's Indian communities, will lead the development of the centre, with every Indian community group in WA able to make use of the facility.

The site for the new centre was secured by ISWA last year, with support from the State Government through a Lotterywest grant.

The Multipurpose Indian Community Centre will be used for events, festivals and activities including education programs, day care for the aged, as well as providing a dedicated space for locals with Indian heritage to come together and celebrate their culture and traditions.

ISWA has also secured Federal funding grants to help complete the project.

The Indian community is one of the largest multicultural communities in Western Australia and one of the fastest growing.

Comments attributed to Premier Mark McGowan:

"The Indian community in Western Australia is vibrant, hard-working, and makes a fantastic contribution to society.

"After attending recent Diwali celebrations, it is clear that this WA community is growing.

"Today's announcement of funding from the State Government will ensure that they will soon have a dedicated community centre to host events, festivals and education programs.

"I'm excited to see this project progress to completion, and look forward to attending events in the coming years."

https://www.wa.gov.au/government/media-statements/McGowan-Labor-Government/McGowan-Labor-Government-contributes-$1.5-million-to-construct-new-... 1/2

Organisation of African Communities in WA[84] -

Africa Day, celebrated annually on May 25th, is a momentous occasion organized by the Organisation of African Communities in Western Australia (OACWA). This event commemorates the founding of the Organisation of African Unity (OAU) in 1963, which later became the African Union (AU), and serves as a celebration of African culture, heritage, and solidarity across the continent and its diaspora.

In Western Australia, Africa Day organized by OACWA is a vibrant and multifaceted event that showcases the rich tapestry of African cultures through music, dance, cuisine, and art. Held in various venues across Perth, the celebration attracts a diverse audience, including members of the African community, local residents, and government officials, fostering cross-cultural understanding and appreciation.

Figure 15 - Organisation of African communities in WA inc

---

84 Extracted from the public domain information available at - https://oacwa.com.au/africaday/

Sri Lankan Cultural Society of Western Australia[85]

The Sri Lankan Cultural Society of Western Australia (SLCWA) is dedicated to promoting and preserving Sri Lankan culture within the region while fostering intercultural understanding and community integration. Established to serve the needs of Sri Lankan expatriates and to share their rich cultural heritage with the broader Western Australian community, the SLCWA engages in a variety of activities and events that highlight the vibrant traditions of Sri Lanka.

One of the society's key initiatives is organizing cultural festivals and events that celebrate traditional Sri Lankan holidays and customs, such as Sinhala and Tamil New Year. These celebrations typically feature traditional music, dance, and cuisine, providing an immersive experience of Sri Lankan culture. The society also hosts educational workshops, language classes, and art exhibitions, which not only educate members of the Sri Lankan diaspora but also invite participation from the wider community.

---

85 Extracted from the public domain information available at - https://www.facebook.com/profile.php?id=100064932150673

Figure 16 - Reflecting the community aspirations

Playing a distint role in community engagement by the various community organisations

In Western Australia, various community organizations cater to the distinct needs of their respective communities, each contributing uniquely to the cultural and social fabric of the region.

The **Indian Society of Western Australia** addresses the needs of the Indian diaspora by fostering a sense of community through cultural celebrations, educational programs, and support services. Their events, such as Diwali and Holi festivals, not only preserve Indian traditions but also provide a platform for cultural exchange and integration with the broader Australian society. Additionally, they offer support services like legal advice, career counseling, and language classes to assist new immigrants in settling into their new environment.

The **Organisation of African Communities in Western Australia (OACWA)** serves a diverse group of African Australians by focusing on cultural preservation, community cohesion, and advocacy. OACWA's activities include organizing African cultural festivals, workshops, and social events that highlight African traditions and foster a sense of belonging among community members. They also work to address the specific needs of African migrants, including support for refugees, youth programs, and initiatives aimed at enhancing socio-economic opportunities within the community.

The **Sri Lankan Cultural Society of Western Australia (SLCWA)** caters to the Sri Lankan community by celebrating their rich cultural heritage through events and activities that promote cultural continuity and integration. The SLCWA organizes traditional festivals like Sinhala and Tamil New Year, offers language classes, and provides a network of support for Sri Lankan immigrants to help them adapt to life in Western Australia. Their focus is on preserving Sri Lankan traditions while facilitating intercultural understanding and community involvement.

Each of these organizations plays a crucial role in meeting the unique needs of their respective communities. They offer cultural preservation, social support, and integration services tailored to their members, contributing to a vibrant and cohesive multicultural environment in Western Australia. Through their dedicated efforts, these organizations help bridge cultural gaps, support new immigrants, and enrich the cultural diversity of the region.

CHAPTER 8

COMMUNITY PARTNERSHIPS

Introduction

This chapter will:
- In the preceding chapter, we explored the complexities and significance of community decision-making, emphasizing its pivotal role and inherent challenges. Building on that foundation, this chapter delves into the essential components of fostering effective community partnerships. While decision-making processes demand collaboration, inclusivity, and effectiveness, partnerships themselves are the bedrock of these principles. This chapter will focus on how to establish and nurture partnerships that embody these core values. As we delve into strategies for creating meaningful and productive collaborations, the central theme of working relationships will once again underscore our discussion, highlighting how strong, well-managed partnerships are crucial for successful community engagement and decision-making.

8.1. Introduction

In community development and community engagement, the concepts of collaboration, partnerships, linkages, and coalitions are often employed interchangeably, reflecting the nuanced ways in which diverse groups work together to address shared objectives. Despite the lack of universally accepted definitions, a common thread unites these terms: they all involve joint action towards mutually agreed-upon goals.

The term "community coalition" specifically refers to a collective of various interest groups that unite their resources—both material and human—to effectuate changes that individual members might struggle to achieve alone. As Brown (1984) highlights, such coalitions are instrumental in tackling complex issues that require a multifaceted approach and broad-based support. This concept underscores the idea that by pooling their strengths, organizations and individuals can overcome barriers that would be insurmountable independently.

Partnerships, in a broader sense, are defined as alliances among people and organizations from different sectors, working together to achieve a common purpose. Himmelman (1992[86]) captures this definition, emphasizing the collaborative nature of partnerships in achieving shared goals through coordinated efforts. This definition highlights the strategic alignment necessary in partnerships, where diverse entities come together, leveraging their distinct strengths and resources to address common challenges effectively.

In the business world, partnerships are similarly characterized by purposive strategic relationships between independent firms. According to Mohr and Spekman (1994), such partnerships are

---

[86] Ibid 61

driven by compatible goals and mutual benefits, where firms acknowledge a high level of interdependence. This definition stresses the importance of shared objectives and mutual reliance, wherein firms collaborate to achieve goals that would be difficult to accomplish individually. This perspective illustrates how strategic partnerships in business mirror the collaborative efforts seen in community settings, where entities work together towards a common aim.

The overarching theme across these definitions is the notion of collaboration towards a shared goal. Whether in community coalitions, partnerships, or business relationships, the focus is on achieving objectives that individual entities alone could not readily attain. Effective partnerships rely on a clear understanding of shared goals, mutual benefits, and a commitment to joint action. They necessitate a high degree of interdependence and trust, ensuring that all parties are invested in the collective outcome.

In practical terms, fostering successful community partnerships involves recognizing the unique contributions of each participant and aligning their efforts towards a common purpose. This collaborative approach not only maximizes the impact of individual contributions but also enhances the overall effectiveness of the initiative. By bringing together diverse perspectives and resources, partnerships can address complex social and health issues more comprehensively than any single entity could manage alone.

In conclusion, while the terms collaboration, partnerships, linkages, and coalitions may be used interchangeably, they all underscore a crucial aspect of community development: the power of collective action. Understanding and implementing these collaborative frameworks allows communities to tackle challenges more effectively, harnessing the strengths of diverse groups to achieve shared goals. The principles of mutual benefit, strategic alignment, and interdependence are central to building and sustaining successful partnerships that drive meaningful change.

Figure 17 - Relationship Types

Relationships are fluid, moving up and down the spectrum depending upon the task and context, and relative impact and intensity of the relationship. The position on the spectrum is also indicative of the expectations and commitments.

Communities partnership framework[87]

8.2. Terms and definitions

Collaboration:
- **Definition**: Joint efforts by multiple parties working together towards shared goals.
- **Focus**: Emphasizes cooperative processes where parties contribute their resources and expertise to achieve a common objective.
- **Usage**: Often used to describe the process of working together, especially in the context of specific projects or initiatives.

Partnerships:
- **Definition**: Alliances among people and organizations from different sectors aiming to achieve common purposes (Himmelman, 1992).
- **Focus**: Strategic relationships that involve mutual benefit and interdependence among parties.
- **Usage**: Applied broadly across various sectors, including community development and business, highlighting long-term, strategic collaborations.

Linkages:
- **Definition**: Connections or relationships between different organizations or entities to facilitate the flow of information or resources.
- **Focus**: Networking and integration of efforts to enhance coordination and support between different parties.

---

[87] Extracted from the Department of Communities – Partnership framework - https://www.wa.gov.au/system/files/2021-05/Communities-Partnership-Framework.pdf

- **Usage**: Often used to describe connections between organizations that help to streamline processes or enhance collaborative efforts.

Coalitions:
- **Definition**: Organizations of diverse interest groups that combine resources to achieve specific changes (Brown, 1984).
- **Focus**: Emphasizes the coalition's role in addressing issues that require collective action and resources.
- **Usage**: Typically refers to temporary or issue-specific alliances formed to tackle particular challenges that individual members cannot address alone.

Understanding these terms is crucial for effective community partnerships. Each term—collaboration, partnerships, linkages, and coalitions—reflects different aspects of how groups work together, whether through direct cooperative actions, strategic alliances, informational connections, or collective efforts aimed at specific changes. Recognizing these nuances helps practitioners design and implement effective community initiatives by leveraging the unique contributions and strengths of each participating entity.

8.3. Effective partnership

Achieving clarity in the purpose of a partnership is foundational to its success and involves a nuanced process of defining and negotiating the roles, skills, experience, and resources that each partner contributes. This clarity is crucial because it establishes the framework within which the partnership operates, ensuring that all parties have a shared understanding of their responsibilities and expectations. Effective partnership negotiation requires careful consideration of the contributions of each partner, and a balanced approach to integrating these diverse elements into a cohesive strategy.

The importance of clearly defining roles and expectations cannot be overstated. Each partner brings unique strengths and resources to the table, which should be leveraged to enhance the partnership's effectiveness. This includes not only understanding what each partner can contribute but also how these contributions will be utilized to achieve the partnership's goals. For instance, a community organization might offer deep local knowledge and grassroots connections, while a government agency might provide funding and policy support. The integration of these diverse resources and perspectives is essential for developing a comprehensive and effective approach to community issues.

However, the process of partnership negotiation is not without its challenges. One of the primary issues is managing power dynamics. As noted by Poland et al. (2005), stronger partners—those with greater resources or influence—can unintentionally dominate the decision-making process. This can lead to an imbalance where the voices of less powerful partners are marginalized. To address this, it is crucial that negotiations are conducted with a focus on equity and inclusion, ensuring that all partners have a fair opportunity to influence the partnership's direction and outcomes. Effective management of power dynamics involves acknowledging existing imbalances and implementing strategies to mitigate their effects.

Disagreement and friction are natural components of partnership work and should be viewed not as barriers but as opportunities for growth and refinement. Williams Labonte (2005[88]) suggests that

---

88 Williams, A., Labonte, R., Randall, J. E., & Muhajarine, N. (2005).

Figure 18 -Partnership lifecycle[1]

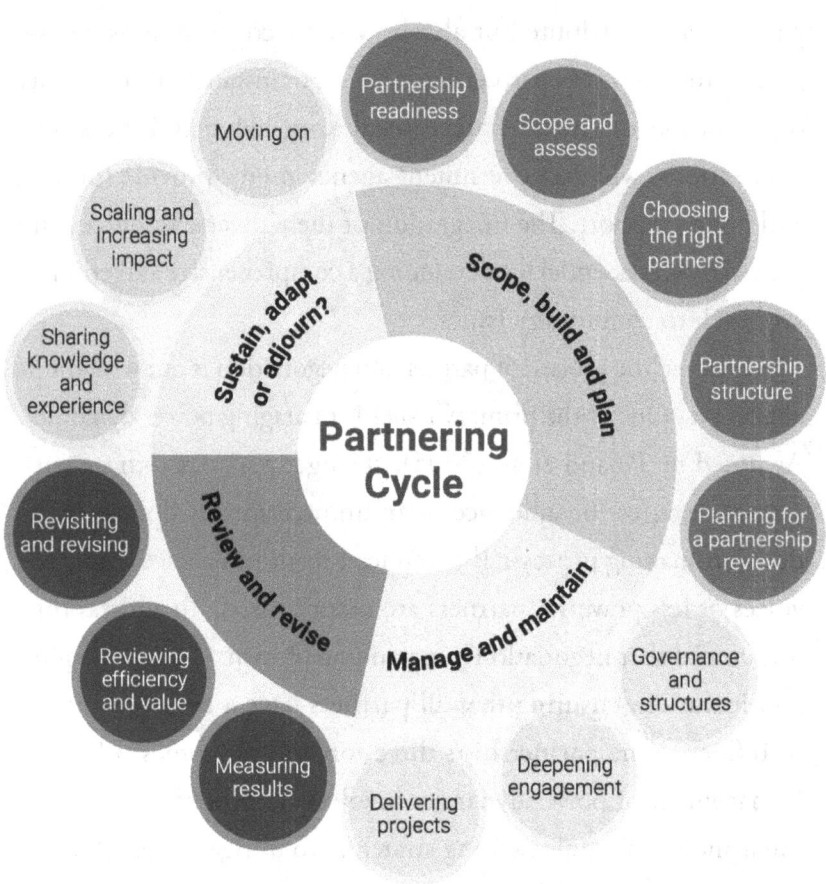

---

1 Extracted from the Department of Communities – Partnership framework - https://www.wa.gov.au/system/files/2021-05/Communities-Partnership-Framework.pdf

conflict and differences can be the driving force behind productive partnership activity. Such friction often highlights underlying issues or divergent perspectives that, when addressed constructively, can lead to more robust and innovative solutions. Embracing disagreement as part of the process can enhance the partnership's resilience and adaptability.

Power imbalances between communities, government agencies, and organizations are common and must be carefully examined. The assumption that power dynamics are static or easily understood can lead to misunderstandings and ineffective partnership functioning. Therefore, it is essential to engage in a thorough exploration of these dynamics to identify who holds power and how it influences the partnership. This involves ongoing dialogue and reflection, as power relationships can shift over time and may affect how decisions are made and how resources are allocated.

The process of clarifying the partnership's purpose is ongoing and dynamic. Initial goals and objectives may need to be adjusted as the partnership evolves and as new needs and challenges arise. This requires regular strategic planning and reassessment to ensure that the partnership remains aligned with its objectives and responsive to changing circumstances. Communities and organizations may sometimes be reluctant to engage in this reassessment process due to concerns about exposing disagreements or unmanaged problems. However, addressing these issues openly is crucial for maintaining the partnership's effectiveness and ensuring that it continues to meet the needs of the community.

In this context, achieving clarity in a partnership involves more

---

Establishing and sustaining community–university partnerships: A case study of quality of life research. *Critical public health*, *15*(3), 291-302.

than defining roles and expectations; it requires careful management of power dynamics, openness to disagreement, and ongoing reassessment of goals. By addressing these aspects thoughtfully and proactively, partnerships can navigate complexities and work more effectively towards their shared objectives. This approach not only enhances the partnership's ability to achieve its goals but also fosters a more equitable and collaborative working environment.

8.4. Partnership types and development

Understanding the dynamics of community partnerships requires a deep appreciation of the interaction patterns that influence how these collaborations function and evolve. The concepts of vertical and horizontal patterning, as articulated by Warren (1978) and further developed by Martinez-Brawley (2000), offer a useful framework for analyzing the potential and challenges of collaborative activities within and outside the community.

Horizontal patterning refers to the relationships and interactions among various social units and sub-systems within a community. These units can include diverse organizations such as sporting clubs, women's groups, and service clubs, each contributing to the community's social fabric. Horizontal interactions are characterized by their internal focus, emphasizing how different community groups collaborate, share resources, and support one another. For example, a local sports club might work with a women's organization to host community events, fostering a sense of unity and shared purpose among different segments of the community. This pattern of interaction is crucial for building a cohesive community, as it facilitates cooperation and resource sharing within the local context.

On the other hand, vertical patterning describes the connections between community social units and external systems, such as relationships between local and state governments. This pattern is crucial for integrating the community with broader governance structures and external resources. Vertical interactions ensure that community needs and priorities are communicated to higher levels of authority, and that external support, such as funding or policy guidance, is effectively utilized. For instance, a neighbourhood health centre might engage in vertical interactions with state health departments to secure funding, access specialized knowledge, and align its services with broader health policies. These connections help the community integrate its local initiatives with regional and national frameworks, facilitating the flow of information and resources that are essential for the sustainability and effectiveness of community projects.

In health and human services projects, achieving a balance between vertical and horizontal patterning is essential. Horizontal interactions within the community enable the project to leverage local knowledge, foster community engagement, and build networks of support. These interactions are dynamic and influenced by the community's power structures and social networks. For instance, community members' relationships with friends, neighbours, and family can impact their willingness to participate in and support health promotion initiatives. Strong horizontal connections can enhance the relevance and acceptance of health projects by ensuring they are tailored to local needs and preferences.

Simultaneously, vertical interactions provide crucial external connections that bring in information about best practices, funding opportunities, and professional expertise. These interactions help community projects stay informed about effective approaches and resources and ensure that they are supported by necessary financial and policy frameworks. In the case of establishing a neighbourhood centre, vertical patterning would involve engaging with local government officials to secure funding and align the centre's objectives with municipal priorities, while also tapping into state-level resources and policies.

The interplay between these two types of patterning—horizontal and vertical—creates a dynamic environment where community initiatives can thrive. Effective partnership development requires recognizing and managing these interactions to maximize their potential. Horizontal relationships foster internal cohesion and collaboration, while vertical connections provide the necessary support and integration with external systems. Balancing these patterns ensures that community projects are not only rooted in local needs but also connected to broader resources and policies, enhancing their impact and sustainability.

Understanding and leveraging both vertical and horizontal patterning is vital for successful partnership development. By navigating these patterns thoughtfully, community practitioners can build more effective, collaborative, and resilient initiatives that address both local and external needs. This holistic approach helps bridge the gap between community-level interactions and broader institutional support, ultimately contributing to more robust and impactful community outcomes.

8.5 Summary

Navigating community partnerships involves understanding and effectively managing the complex interplay between various types of interactions and relationships that influence collaborative efforts. This chapter delves into the dynamics of community partnerships, emphasizing the importance of both horizontal and vertical patterning as outlined by Warren (1978) and Martinez-Brawley (2000).

Horizontal patterning pertains to the interactions among community-based social units and sub-systems, such as sporting groups, women's organizations, and local service clubs. These relationships are vital for fostering cooperation, resource sharing, and support within the community. They represent the internal dynamics that drive local cohesion and collective action. For instance, local organizations may work together on community events or initiatives, strengthening bonds and building a unified approach to addressing local needs.

Vertical patterning, on the other hand, refers to the connections between community entities and external systems, such as local, state, and national governments. These interactions are crucial for integrating community efforts with broader governance structures and accessing external resources. Vertical patterning ensures that community needs and priorities are communicated to higher levels of authority and that projects are supported by necessary funding, policy guidance, and expert knowledge.

Balancing these two types of patterning is essential for the success of community partnerships. Horizontal interactions ensure that community projects are grounded in local needs and supported by strong internal networks. They enable community members to collaborate and build relationships that enhance the relevance and acceptance of initiatives. Vertical interactions provide the necessary external support, including financial resources, policy alignment, and access to broader expertise. They help ensure that community projects are informed by best practices and integrated into larger systems.

Effective partnership development requires careful management of both horizontal and vertical interactions. Practitioners must navigate the complexities of internal community dynamics while also establishing and maintaining connections with external entities. This dual approach helps to create robust, collaborative, and sustainable initiatives that address both local and broader needs.

In summary, navigating community partnerships involves a comprehensive understanding of how horizontal and vertical patterning influences collaboration and effectiveness. By managing these interactions thoughtfully, community practitioners can enhance the impact and sustainability of their initiatives, ensuring that community efforts are both locally relevant and well-supported by external systems. This holistic approach is essential for building effective, resilient partnerships that contribute to positive community outcomes.

NEW ROOTS

Figure 19 - Partnership Analysis checklist

The checklist

Rate your level of agreement with each of the statements below, with 1 indicating strong disagreement and 5 indicating strong agreement. The scores will be totalled automatically. To save your checklist, select 'File'/'Save As'/'PDF'. You can then name your checklist and email it to your partner organisations as an attachment.

	1 Strongly disagree	2 Disagree	3 Not sure	4 Agree	5 Strongly agree	
1. Determining the need for the partnership						
There is a perceived need for the partnership in terms of areas of common interest and complementary capacity.	○	○	○	○	○	
There is a clear goal for the partnership.	○	○	○	○	○	
There is a shared understanding of, and commitment to, this goal among all potential partners.	○	○	○	○	○	
The partners are willing to share some of their ideas, resources, influence and power to fulfil the goal.	○	○	○	○	○	
The perceived benefits of the partnership outweigh the perceived costs.	○	○	○	○	○	SUBTOTAL
SUBTOTAL						0
2. Choosing partners						
The partners share common ideologies, interests and approaches.	○	○	○	○	○	
The partners see their core business as partially interdependent.	○	○	○	○	○	
There is a history of good relations between the partners.	○	○	○	○	○	
The partnership brings added prestige to the partners individually as well as collectively.	○	○	○	○	○	
There is enough variety among members to have a comprehensive understanding of the issues being addressed.	○	○	○	○	○	SUBTOTAL
SUBTOTAL						0
3. Making sure partnerships work						
The managers in each organisation (or division) support the partnership.	○	○	○	○	○	
Partners have the necessary skills for collaborative action.	○	○	○	○	○	
There are strategies to enhance the skills of the partnership through increasing the membership or workforce development.	○	○	○	○	○	
The roles, responsibilities and expectations of partners are clearly defined and understood by all other partners.	○	○	○	○	○	
The administrative, communication and decision-making structure of the partnership is as simple as possible.	○	○	○	○	○	SUBTOTAL
SUBTOTAL						0
4. Planning collaborative action						
All partners are involved in planning and setting priorities for collaborative action.	○	○	○	○	○	
Partners have the task of communicating and promoting the partnership in their own organisations.	○	○	○	○	○	
Some staff have roles that cross the traditional boundaries that exist between agencies or divisions in the partnership.	○	○	○	○	○	
The lines of communication, roles and expectations of partners are clear.	○	○	○	○	○	
There is a participatory decision-making system that is accountable, responsive and inclusive.	○	○	○	○	○	SUBTOTAL
SUBTOTAL						0

	1 Strongly disagree	2 Disagree	3 Not sure	4 Agree	5 Strongly agree
5. Implementing collaborative action					
Processes that are common across agencies have been standardised (e.g. referral protocols, service standards, data collection and reporting mechanisms).	O	O	O	O	O
There is an investment in the partnership of time, personnel, materials or facilities.	O	O	O	O	O
Collaborative action by staff and reciprocity between agencies is rewarded by management.	O	O	O	O	O
The action is adding value (rather than duplicating services) for the community, clients or agencies involved in the partnership.	O	O	O	O	O
There are regular opportunities for informal and voluntary contact between staff from the different agencies and other members of the partnership.	O	O	O	O	O
SUBTOTAL					SUBTOTAL 0
6. Minimising the barriers to partnerships					
Differences in organisational priorities, goals and tasks have been addressed.	O	O	O	O	O
There is a core group of skilled and committed (in terms of the partnership) staff that has continued over the life of the partnership.	O	O	O	O	O
There are formal structures for sharing information and resolving demarcation disputes.	O	O	O	O	O
There are informal ways of achieving this.	O	O	O	O	O
There are strategies to ensure alternative views are expressed within the partnership.	O	O	O	O	O
SUBTOTAL					SUBTOTAL 0
7. Reflecting on and continuing the partnership					
There are processes for recognising and celebrating collective achievements and/or individual contributions.	O	O	O	O	O
The partnership can demonstrate or document the outcomes of its collective work.	O	O	O	O	O
There is a clear need for and commitment to continuing the collaboration in the medium term.	O	O	O	O	O
There are resources available from either internal or external sources to continue the partnership.	O	O	O	O	O
There is a way of reviewing the range of partners and bringing in new members or removing some.	O	O	O	O	O
SUBTOTAL					SUBTOTAL 0

Aggregate score	TOTAL
1. Determining the need for the partnership	0
2. Choosing partners	0
3. Making sure partnerships work	0
4. Planning collaborative action	0
5. Implementing collaborative action	0
6. Minimising the barriers to partnerships	0
7. Reflecting on and continuing the partnership	0

CHAPTER 9

COMMUNITY PLANNING

In community planning, several critical elements must be integrated to create effective and responsive strategies. This chapter builds on the foundational aspects of decision-making, leadership, and partnership formation, which are essential for successful community planning. It also emphasizes the importance of measuring and building community capacity, as outlined in Chapter 2.

Introduction

This chapter includes:
- **Integration of Decision-Making and Leadership:** Effective community planning relies heavily on the processes of decision-making and leadership discussed in earlier chapters. These elements help guide the planning process, ensuring that strategies are well-informed and aligned with community needs.
- **Formation of Partnerships**: Building and maintaining partnerships is crucial in community planning. Collaborations with

various stakeholders, including community members, organizations, and government agencies, enhance the planning process by bringing diverse perspectives and resources to the table.
- **Techniques for Community Planning**: The chapter describes several useful techniques for community planning, including:
  - **Rapid Appraisal**: This technique, as discussed by Ong et al. (1991), allows for quick assessment of community needs and resources through focused and efficient data collection methods.
  - **Service Audit**: Conducting a service audit helps identify existing services, gaps, and areas for improvement, providing a comprehensive view of community service provision.
  - **Delphi Survey Technique**: This method involves collecting expert opinions through multiple rounds of surveys to achieve consensus on community issues and solutions.
- **Community Health Profile:** The chapter also focuses on building a community health profile, a technique detailed by Rissel and Bracht (1999). This process involves gathering and analyzing data related to the health status of a community, which helps in identifying health needs, setting priorities, and developing targeted interventions.

In summary, effective community planning is a multifaceted process that incorporates decision-making, leadership, partnerships, and specific planning techniques. By integrating these elements and employing methods such as rapid appraisal, service audits, and the Delphi survey technique, practitioners can develop comprehensive plans that address community needs and enhance overall well-being.

9.1. Introduction

Community planning is a comprehensive process that integrates various elements to create effective, responsive strategies for community development. This chapter delves into how the principles of decision-making, leadership, and partnership formation, discussed in previous chapters, converge in the realm of community planning. It also introduces several practical techniques that can enhance the planning process and details two specific types of community planning that are crucial for understanding and improving community health and services.

The Integration of Decision-Making, Leadership, and Partnerships

Community planning is fundamentally shaped by the decision-making processes, leadership strategies, and partnership formations that underpin its success. Effective decision-making is at the heart of community planning, requiring practitioners to use evidence-based approaches and inclusive practices to address community needs. This involves not only gathering and analyzing data but also engaging with diverse stakeholders to ensure that all voices are heard and considered.

Leadership plays a pivotal role in guiding the community planning process. Leaders must be able to inspire and mobilize community members and partners, providing vision and direction while navigating complex dynamics and potential conflicts. Strong leadership facilitates the alignment of community goals with actionable plans, ensuring that initiatives are both feasible and sustainable.

Partnerships are equally critical in community planning. Collaborative efforts between community organizations, local government, and other stakeholders help pool resources, share expertise, and enhance the overall effectiveness of planning efforts. Forming and maintaining these partnerships requires ongoing communication, mutual respect, and a shared commitment to common objectives.

Techniques for Community Planning

Several techniques are instrumental in the community planning process, each contributing to a more thorough understanding of community needs and resources.

Rapid appraisal, as discussed by Ong et al. (1991), is a technique designed for quick and effective assessment of community conditions. This approach involves using focused and efficient data collection methods to rapidly gather information about community needs, resources, and priorities. By utilizing rapid appraisal, practitioners can gain a snapshot of the community's situation, which is particularly useful when time or resources are limited.

Conducting a service audit is another valuable technique in community planning. This process involves systematically reviewing existing services within a community to identify gaps, redundancies, and areas for improvement. A service audit provides a clear picture of what services are available, how they are being used, and where additional support might be needed. This information is crucial for planning initiatives that aim to address unmet needs and enhance service delivery.

The Delphi survey technique is also highlighted as a method for gathering expert opinions and reaching consensus on community issues. This technique involves a series of surveys with experts who provide input on specific topics. Through multiple rounds of feedback, practitioners can refine their understanding of community needs and develop strategies based on expert consensus. The Delphi method is particularly useful for addressing complex issues where expert knowledge and foresight are essential.

Building a Community Health Profile

Two specific types of community planning receive particular attention in this chapter: building a community health profile and its relevance for health promotion. Rissel[89] and Bracht (1999[90]) emphasize the importance of creating a comprehensive community health profile to better understand the health status and needs of a community. This process involves collecting and analyzing data on various health indicators, such as disease prevalence, access to healthcare services, and social determinants of health.

By constructing a detailed community health profile, practitioners can identify key health issues, prioritize areas for intervention, and design targeted health promotion strategies. This profile not only informs the development of health initiatives but also helps in assessing the effectiveness of existing programs and making necessary adjustments.

Community planning is an intricate process that requires the integration of decision-making, leadership, and partnership strategies. Techniques such as rapid appraisal, service audits, and the Delphi survey method enhance the planning process by

---

89 Rissel, C., Bracht, n. (1999), 'Assessing community needs, resources and readiness', in N.Bracht (ed.) *Health Promotion at the Community Level-2-New Advance,* Sage Publications Inc., Thousand Oaks, California, pp.59-69

90 Bracht, N. & Tsouros, A. (1990). 'Principles and Strategies of Effective Community Participation', *Health Promotion International,* Vol. 5, No. 3, pp. 199-208

providing valuable insights and facilitating informed decision-making. Building a community health profile is a crucial component of planning, enabling practitioners to develop targeted interventions and improve overall community health. Through a comprehensive approach that combines these elements, community planning can effectively address needs, leverage resources, and foster positive change within communities.

9.2. Social Justice and Human rights perspective
In Community development and planning, social justice and human rights are fundamental principles that guide ethical practice and ensure that all individuals have equitable access to opportunities and resources. This chapter delves into how a social justice and human rights perspective shapes community work, the implications of these principles for community planning and development, and the strategies for integrating them into practice.

Understanding Social Justice and Human Rights
Social justice and human rights are interconnected concepts that address the distribution of resources, opportunities, and privileges within society. Social justice refers to the fair and equitable distribution of benefits and burdens, ensuring that all individuals have access to the resources necessary for their well-being and development. It seeks to address and rectify inequalities, discrimination, and systemic barriers that hinder individuals from fully participating in society.

Human rights, on the other hand, are universal entitlements that every individual possesses by virtue of their humanity. These rights include civil, political, economic, social, and cultural rights, as enshrined in international declarations and treaties such as the Universal Declaration of Human Rights. Human rights principles underpin the idea that every person deserves respect, dignity, and equal treatment regardless of their background, identity, or circumstances.

Incorporating Social Justice and Human Rights into Community Planning

Incorporating social justice and human rights into community planning involves several key practices and considerations. First and foremost, community planners must ensure that their initiatives are inclusive and equitable, actively working to address disparities and barriers faced by marginalized or disadvantaged groups. This requires a thorough understanding of the social and economic context of the community, including the various forms of inequality and discrimination that may be present.

A critical aspect of applying a social justice perspective is engaging with diverse community members and stakeholders to understand their needs, experiences, and aspirations. This engagement should be genuine and meaningful, ensuring that all voices are heard and that decisions reflect the collective input of the community. Practitioners should strive to create spaces where marginalized groups, such as people of color, individuals with disabilities, and low-income populations, can participate actively and influence the planning process.

Furthermore, community planning should be guided by principles of equity and fairness. This involves designing programs and policies that not only address immediate needs but also tackle the root causes of inequality and injustice. For example, when planning a new community health initiative, practitioners should consider how the program will impact different segments of the population, particularly those who are most vulnerable or underserved. Ensuring that resources are allocated in a way that promotes equitable access and addresses disparities is crucial for advancing social justice.

Strategies for Implementing Social Justice and Human Rights Principles

To effectively integrate social justice and human rights principles into community planning, several strategies can be employed. One important strategy is to conduct comprehensive needs assessments that highlight the specific challenges and barriers faced by different groups within the community. This assessment should include both quantitative data and qualitative insights gathered through consultations, interviews, and focus groups with community members.

Another key strategy is to adopt a rights-based approach to planning and development. This approach involves framing community issues and initiatives within the context of human rights, ensuring that all actions are aligned with the principles of dignity, respect, and equality. Practitioners can use human rights frameworks to assess the impact of their projects, develop accountability mechanisms, and advocate for policies that uphold human rights standards.

Capacity building is also essential for promoting social justice and human rights. This involves empowering community members and organizations with the knowledge, skills, and resources needed to advocate for their rights and participate effectively in decision-making processes. Training and education programs can help raise awareness about human rights and social justice issues, equipping individuals with the tools to address injustices and promote equitable outcomes.

Challenges and Considerations

Implementing a social justice and human rights perspective in community planning is not without its challenges. Practitioners may encounter resistance from stakeholders who are reluctant to confront issues of inequality or who prioritize other goals over social justice. Navigating these challenges requires a commitment to advocacy, persistence, and the ability to build alliances with like-minded individuals and organizations.

Moreover, ensuring that social justice and human rights principles are embedded in community planning requires ongoing reflection and adaptation. Practitioners must be prepared to reassess their approaches, address emerging issues, and adjust strategies based on feedback and changing circumstances. This dynamic process involves a continual commitment to learning, growth, and responsiveness to the needs of the community.

In summary, a social justice and human rights perspective is essential for guiding community planning and development practices. By prioritizing equity, inclusivity, and respect for human rights, practitioners can create more effective and just initiatives that address the needs of all community members. Integrating these principles into practice involves engaging with diverse stakeholders, using rights-based frameworks, and addressing systemic inequalities, while remaining mindful of the challenges and complexities inherent in this work. Through a steadfast commitment to social justice and human rights, community practitioners can contribute to building more equitable and inclusive communities.

9.3. A Community profile

A community profile is a vital tool in community planning that provides a comprehensive snapshot of a community's health, strengths, and needs. This chapter explores the purpose and components of a community health profile, highlighting how it can be used to inform decision-making and strategic planning. Drawing on Nelson (2001), this chapter details the key elements typically included in a community profile, examining their significance and application.

Demographic Information

Demographic information forms the foundation of a community profile. It provides essential insights into the composition of the community, including data on age, gender, ethnicity, socioeconomic status, and other relevant characteristics. Understanding these demographic aspects helps practitioners identify the specific needs and preferences of different population groups. For instance, age distribution data can inform decisions about services and programs for children, adults, or seniors. Ethnic and cultural data are crucial for ensuring that initiatives are culturally appropriate and accessible to all community members.

Status Information

Status information encompasses data routinely collected at various levels—local, regional, and national—that reflects the current conditions and trends within the community. This information is integral to assessing the overall health and well-being of the population. The key areas typically covered include:

- **Participation**: This refers to the level of community engagement and involvement in local activities, decision-making processes, and programs. High participation rates often indicate strong community engagement and support for initiatives. Conversely, low participation may highlight barriers to involvement or a lack of interest, which can be addressed through targeted strategies.
- **Leadership**: Understanding the leadership structures within the community is crucial for effective planning. This includes identifying key leaders, their roles, and how they influence decision-making and resource allocation. Effective leadership can drive positive change, while weak or fragmented leadership may hinder progress.
- **Organisational Structures**: This component examines the various organizations operating within the community, including non-profits, community groups, and service providers. It helps map out the existing infrastructure, collaboration mechanisms, and areas where additional support or coordination may be needed.
- **Problem Assessments**: Identifying and evaluating community problems is essential for targeting interventions effectively. This involves analyzing data on prevalent health issues, social challenges, and other areas of concern. Problem assessments help prioritize needs and allocate resources where they are most required.
- **Resource Mobilization**: Resource mobilization involves identifying and leveraging financial, human, and material resources available within the community. This includes funding sources, volunteer support, and in-kind contributions. Effective resource mobilization ensures that community initiatives are adequately supported and sustainable.

- **Links with Others**: This aspect examines the connections between the community and external organizations, agencies, and networks. Strong links can facilitate collaboration, information sharing, and access to additional resources and expertise. Weak or underdeveloped links may limit opportunities for community development and support.
- **Role of Outside Agents**: Outside agents, such as government bodies, consultants, and non-governmental organizations, play a significant role in community development. Understanding their involvement, contributions, and impact helps assess how external factors influence community planning and outcomes.
- **Programme Management**: Effective program management is crucial for the successful implementation of community initiatives. This includes planning, execution, monitoring, and evaluation of programs. Assessing program management practices helps identify strengths and areas for improvement, ensuring that initiatives are delivered effectively and achieve desired outcomes.

Application of Community Profiles

The information gathered through a community profile is instrumental in guiding community planning and decision-making. By providing a detailed overview of the community's health, resources, and needs, a community profile enables practitioners to:

1. **Identify Priorities**: The data helps determine the most pressing issues and areas requiring attention. This allows for targeted interventions that address specific community needs and enhance overall well-being.
2. **Develop Strategies**: With a clear understanding of community

dynamics, practitioners can design and implement strategies that are tailored to the local context. This includes developing programs that align with community needs, leveraging existing resources, and addressing gaps in services.

3. **Monitor Progress**: Community profiles serve as a baseline for measuring progress over time. By regularly updating and reviewing the profile, practitioners can track changes, evaluate the impact of interventions, and make necessary adjustments to strategies.
4. **Facilitate Collaboration**: The profile helps identify potential partners and collaborators, both within and outside the community. Building strong partnerships and networks can enhance the effectiveness of community initiatives and support collective efforts.
5. **Advocate for Resources**: Comprehensive community profiles provide a compelling case for securing funding and resources. By demonstrating the community's needs and potential, practitioners can advocate for additional support and investment.

In summary, a community profile is a comprehensive tool that integrates various types of information to provide a holistic view of a community's health and needs. By incorporating demographic data and status information, practitioners can effectively plan, implement, and evaluate community initiatives, ensuring that they are responsive to the community's unique context and challenges. The insights gained from a community profile are essential for driving positive change and fostering sustainable development.

9.4. Techniques for community planning

Community planning involves a range of methods and techniques aimed at understanding and addressing the needs of a community effectively. One prominent technique that has proven valuable in various settings is Rapid Appraisal (RA). This chapter explores Rapid Appraisal, its characteristics, and its application in community planning.

A) Rapid Appraisal (RA)

Rapid Appraisal (RA) is a methodological approach used in both rural and urban community settings to gather and analyze information quickly and efficiently. RA is also known by other terms such as Participatory Rural Appraisal (PRA) and Rapid Rural Appraisal (RRA). Although these terms are used interchangeably, the core principles of RA are consistently applied to obtain timely and relevant insights.

Characteristics of Rapid Appraisal

1. **Speed Compared to Conventional Methods**: One of the defining features of RA is its emphasis on speed. Unlike traditional methods of analysis, which may involve lengthy and detailed processes, RA is designed to provide insights rapidly. This allows practitioners to respond to community needs and issues promptly, making it particularly useful in dynamic or urgent situations.

2. **Field-Based Work**: RA involves working directly 'in the field,' meaning that practitioners engage with community members in their own environments. This direct interaction facilitates a deeper understanding of the community's context, needs, and

resources. Field-based work ensures that the data collected is grounded in the real-world experiences of the community.

3. **Learning Directly from Local Inhabitants**: The approach emphasizes learning directly from the local inhabitants rather than relying solely on secondary data or external experts. By engaging with community members, practitioners gain first-hand insights into local conditions, priorities, and challenges. This participatory approach helps ensure that the information gathered is relevant and reflective of the community's true situation. 'Participatory Rural Appraisal' (PRA) (Gona et al, 2006[91]) and 'Rapid Rural Appraisal' (RRA) (Melville, 1993[92])

4. **Semi-Structured, Multidisciplinary Approach**: RA employs a semi-structured approach that allows for flexibility and innovation. Practitioners use a range of methods and techniques, adapting them as needed to fit the specific context of the community. This multidisciplinary approach encourages collaboration between different experts and stakeholders, enriching the analysis and outcomes.

5. **Emphasis on Timely Insights**: Rather than aiming for definitive answers or fixed recommendations, RA focuses on producing timely insights, hypotheses, or 'best bets.' This pragmatic approach recognizes that while RA may not provide final truths, it can offer valuable and actionable information that guides decision-making and planning.

---

91 Gona, J.K., Hartley, S., Newton, J. (2006), 'Using participatory rural appraisal (PRA) in the identification of children with disabilities in rural kilifi, Kenya'. *Rural and Remote Health 6:* <http: rrh.deakin.edu.au>

92 Melville, B. (1993). 'Rapid rural appraisal: Its role in health planning in developing countries', *Tropical Doctor,* Vol. 23, pp. 55-8

Application of Rapid Appraisal in Community Planning

Rapid Appraisal is particularly effective in socio-economically deprived communities where conventional methods may be too slow or resource-intensive (Gona et al, 2006[93]). Its application in community planning involves several key steps:

1. **Engagement with the Community**: Practitioners begin by engaging with community members through various participatory techniques. This may include interviews, focus groups, workshops, and observational studies. The goal is to gather diverse perspectives and understand the community's needs and resources.

2. **Data Collection and Analysis**: Data is collected rapidly using both qualitative and quantitative methods. The analysis focuses on identifying key issues, patterns, and relationships within the community. This may involve mapping resources, assessing needs, and evaluating existing programs.

3. **Development of Insights and Recommendations**: Based on the data collected, practitioners develop insights and preliminary recommendations. These are often presented as hypotheses or 'best bets' rather than final solutions. The emphasis is on providing actionable information that can guide further planning and decision-making.

4. **Feedback and Iteration**: RA is not a one-time process but rather an iterative approach. Practitioners regularly engage with the community to validate findings, refine recommendations, and adjust strategies as needed. This ongoing feedback loop helps ensure that the planning process remains responsive and relevant.

---

[93] Ibid 92

5. **Integration with Broader Planning Efforts**: Insights gained from RA are integrated into broader community planning efforts. This involves aligning findings with existing plans, strategies, and resources. RA helps inform and enhance planning processes by providing a rapid and grounded understanding of community dynamics.

RA is a comprehensive approach to community planning developed in relatively socio-economically deprived communities. This can specifically apply to migrant communities with less societal connections to the broader Australian community.

i. Preparation (3-5 days): facilitators play a crucial role in guiding potential participants through the planning process. They are responsible for providing clear and comprehensive information about the purpose of the planning and the anticipated outcomes. By sensitizing participants to these aspects, facilitators help ensure that everyone understands the goals of the process and is prepared to contribute effectively. This approach not only fosters a collaborative environment but also enhances the likelihood of achieving the desired results from the planning efforts.

ii. Data-gathering (4-6 Days): various methods are employed to gather information, such as workshops, interviews, non-participant observation, and the collection of written records. These approaches allow for a comprehensive understanding of the community's needs and perspectives. Through these methods, participants are encouraged to 'picture' their community and articulate their vision for its development. This process helps ensure that the planning is grounded in the actual experiences and aspirations of the community members, leading to more relevant and effective outcomes.

iii. Synthesis (1-2 days): facilitators, alongside elected community representatives, organize the collected information into broad issue categories—such as education, health, and transport. This categorization helps to structure the data in a way that is accessible and meaningful for further discussion. The categorized information is then presented to the community for review. During this stage, community members could engage in discussions, suggest modifications, and verify the accuracy of the information. This collaborative approach ensures that the community's perspectives are integrated into the planning process, enhancing the relevance and effectiveness of the outcomes.

iv. Ranking (1-2 Days): Workshop participants work closely with key stakeholders to prioritize issues that are of significant importance. This collaborative process helps to identify and focus on the most critical areas for development. When participants and key stakeholders engage in negotiations and discussions together, it fosters a shared sense of ownership and commitment to the proposed changes. This joint effort not only enhances the relevance of the priorities but also increases the likelihood of successful implementation, as both parties are more invested in the outcomes.

v. Preparing and adopting a community action plan (3-4 days): Participants develop the plan by devising strategies to address the identified issues. Once the plan is prepared, it is presented to the broader community and service providers. This presentation allows for further input and feedback, ensuring that the strategies are aligned with the needs and expectations of all stakeholders involved. Engaging both the community and service providers in this review process helps to refine the plan and fosters greater support and collaboration for its implementation.

vi. Implementation and monitoring: Finally the initiative is carried out by governmental agencies, various joint committees comprising both governmental and non-governmental organizations, and local community workers. These collaborative efforts ensure a comprehensive approach to addressing the issues at hand, leveraging the expertise and resources of all involved parties. By working together, these groups can effectively coordinate their efforts, integrate diverse perspectives, and enhance the overall impact of the initiative.

Service Audits

Service audits are a vital tool in community planning and development, designed to systematically review and assess the effectiveness, efficiency, and coverage of services within a community. This chapter delves into the purpose, process, and benefits of service audits, illustrating how they contribute to better decision-making and resource allocation in community settings.

Purpose and Importance of Service Audits

The primary aim of a service audit is to provide a clear and comprehensive picture of the existing services available within a community. This includes understanding what services are being offered, who is providing them, how they are utilized, and where there may be gaps or redundancies. The insights gained from a service audit are crucial for several reasons:

1. **Identifying Gaps and Redundancies:** By evaluating the range of services provided, practitioners can identify areas where services are lacking or where there may be an overlap. For example, a community might have multiple programs addressing similar needs but no services available for other crucial areas. Recognizing these gaps and redundancies allows for more targeted and efficient service planning and development.
2. **Improving Service Delivery:** Service audits help assess how well existing services meet the needs of the community. This evaluation can reveal issues related to accessibility, quality, and responsiveness. For instance, if certain services are underutilized, it might indicate problems with awareness, accessibility, or service design. Addressing these issues can enhance the overall effectiveness and efficiency of service delivery.
3. **Resource Allocation:** Understanding the distribution and utilization of services helps in making informed decisions about resource allocation. This includes financial resources, personnel, and materials. A service audit can highlight which areas are over- or under-resourced, enabling more equitable and strategic distribution of resources to better serve the community's needs.
4. **Strategic Planning:** The information gathered from a service audit informs strategic planning by providing a factual basis for decision-making. It helps practitioners develop or refine service plans, set priorities, and design interventions based on actual service patterns and community needs.

Process of Conducting a Service Audit

Conducting a service audit involves several key steps, each aimed at gathering and analyzing relevant data to evaluate the effectiveness of services. Here's a detailed look at the typical process:

1. **Planning and Preparation:** The first step in a service audit is to define the scope and objectives of the audit. This involves identifying which services will be reviewed, the criteria for evaluation, and the goals of the audit. Planning also includes assembling a team of auditors and developing a timeline for the audit process.
2. **Data Collection:** The next step involves collecting data on the services being offered. This can be done through various methods, including surveys, interviews with service providers, focus groups with service users, and reviewing existing records and reports. The data collection process should be comprehensive, capturing details about the types of services, their reach, usage patterns, user satisfaction, and any issues or challenges faced.
3. **Data Analysis:** Once the data is collected, it is analyzed to identify patterns, strengths, weaknesses, and areas for improvement. This analysis may involve comparing service provision against community needs, evaluating service effectiveness and efficiency, and assessing the adequacy of resources and support.
4. **Reporting:** The findings from the data analysis are compiled into a report that summarizes the key insights, conclusions, and recommendations. The report should be clear and accessible, highlighting critical issues and providing actionable suggestions for addressing identified gaps and improving service delivery.
5. **Review and Action:** After the report is completed, it is important to review the findings with relevant stakeholders, including service providers, community members, and decision-makers. This review process helps ensure that the recommendations are practical and can be effectively implemented. Based on the

audit results, action plans are developed to address the identified issues and enhance service provision.

Benefits of Service Audits

Service audits offer numerous benefits to community planning and development. They provide a structured approach to evaluating and improving services, helping ensure that community needs are met efficiently and effectively. By identifying gaps, reducing redundancies, and optimizing resource allocation, service audits contribute to more responsive and equitable service delivery. Additionally, they support strategic planning by providing a solid evidence base for decision-making and help foster collaboration among service providers and stakeholders.

In summary, service audits are an essential component of community planning that provide valuable insights into the current state of service provision. Through a systematic process of planning, data collection, analysis, and reporting, service audits help identify and address service gaps, improve delivery, and guide strategic planning efforts. By leveraging the findings from service audits, practitioners can enhance community services, ensure resources are effectively utilized, and better meet the needs of the community.

b) Delphi technique

Rapid Appraisal is a valuable technique for community planning, offering a swift and effective means of understanding and addressing community needs. Its emphasis on field-based work, direct learning from community members, and flexibility in approach makes it well-suited for dynamic and resource-constrained environments. By providing timely insights and fostering participatory engagement,

RA supports informed decision-making and enhances the overall effectiveness of community planning efforts.

The Delphi technique is a systematic, interactive method used to gather expert opinions and achieve a consensus on a particular issue or problem. Originally developed for forecasting and decision-making in various fields, the Delphi technique has been adapted for use in community planning to harness the collective wisdom of experts and stakeholders. This chapter delves into the Delphi technique, detailing its steps and applications, as outlined by Hasson et al. (2000)[94].

Introduction to the Delphi Technique

The Delphi technique is characterized by its iterative process, which involves multiple rounds of surveys or questionnaires to refine and converge on expert opinions. The primary goal is to achieve a consensus on complex issues where uncertainty exists and diverse perspectives need to be considered. The method is particularly useful in community planning for addressing multifaceted problems and developing strategic plans based on informed expert judgment.

Steps in the Delphi Technique

1. **Selection of Experts**: The first step in the Delphi technique involves identifying and selecting a panel of experts who possess relevant knowledge and experience related to the topic under investigation. These experts can come from various fields, including academia, practice, and policy, and should be chosen

---

[94] Hasson, F., Keeney, S., McKenna, H. (2000). 'Research guidance for the Delphi survey technique', *Journal of Advanced Nursing*, Vol. 32, No. 4, pp. 1008-15

based on their expertise and ability to contribute valuable insights. The diversity of the panel ensures a broad range of perspectives and reduces the potential for bias.
2. **Development of the Initial Questionnaire**: Once the panel is assembled, the next step is to develop the initial questionnaire or survey. This questionnaire is designed to gather the experts' opinions on the specific issue or problem being addressed. It typically includes a series of open-ended or structured questions aimed at eliciting detailed responses. The questionnaire should be carefully crafted to ensure clarity and relevance, and it should address the key aspects of the problem.
3. **Distribution and Collection of Responses**: The initial questionnaire is distributed to the panel members, who are asked to provide their responses within a specified timeframe. The responses are collected and analyzed to identify common themes, areas of agreement, and points of divergence. This step is crucial for understanding the range of expert opinions and for preparing the subsequent rounds of the Delphi process.
4. **Analysis and Synthesis of Responses**: After collecting the responses, the next step involves analyzing and synthesizing the data. This process includes summarizing the key findings, identifying trends, and highlighting areas of consensus and disagreement. The goal is to distill the information into meaningful insights that can guide the development of the next round of questions.
5. **Development and Distribution of Follow-Up Questionnaires**: Based on the analysis of the initial responses, a follow-up questionnaire is developed. This questionnaire is designed to refine and clarify the issues raised in the first round and to address

any areas of disagreement. The follow-up questions may be more focused and specific, reflecting the insights gained from the previous round.

6. **Iterative Rounds of Surveying**: The Delphi technique involves multiple rounds of surveying, with each round building on the previous one. After distributing the follow-up questionnaire, the responses are again collected and analyzed. The process is repeated for as many rounds as necessary to achieve a consensus or to reach a satisfactory level of agreement among the experts. Each round helps to refine the issues, reduce uncertainty, and clarify the areas of consensus.

7. **Final Analysis and Report**: Once the final round of the Delphi process is complete, the data is analyzed to summarize the consensus achieved by the panel. A final report is prepared, which includes the key findings, areas of agreement, and any remaining points of divergence. The report provides a comprehensive overview of the expert opinions and offers recommendations based on the collective judgment of the panel.

8. **Feedback and Implementation**: The final report is shared with the panel members and other relevant stakeholders for feedback. This feedback helps to validate the findings and ensure that the recommendations are practical and applicable. The results of the Delphi technique are then used to inform decision-making and planning processes, guiding community initiatives and strategies.

Applications of the Delphi Technique in Community Planning
In community planning, the Delphi technique can be applied to a range of issues, such as assessing community needs, developing

strategic plans, and evaluating program effectiveness. By leveraging the expertise of diverse stakeholders, the Delphi technique helps to ensure that planning efforts are informed by comprehensive and nuanced perspectives. It is particularly useful in situations where there is uncertainty or complexity, as it provides a structured approach to synthesizing expert opinions and reaching a consensus.

The Delphi technique's iterative nature allows for ongoing refinement and adjustment, making it a flexible tool for addressing evolving community needs. Its emphasis on expert judgment and collective input supports evidence-based decision-making and enhances the overall effectiveness of community planning efforts.

Conclusion

The Delphi technique is a valuable method for community planning, offering a systematic approach to gathering and synthesizing expert opinions. By following the steps outlined by Hasson et al. (2000)[95], practitioners can effectively leverage the collective wisdom of a diverse panel to address complex issues, develop strategic plans, and guide community initiatives. The Delphi technique's iterative process and emphasis on consensus-building make it a powerful tool for informed and collaborative decision-making in community planning.

9.5. Summary

Community planning is a multifaceted process that involves various techniques to effectively address and respond to community needs. This chapter focuses on three prominent techniques—Rapid Appraisal, service audits, and the Delphi technique—each of which offers unique advantages for enhancing community planning.

---

95 Ibid 95

Rapid Appraisal (RA) is a technique designed for swift and effective community assessment. It is known by other names such as Participatory Rural Appraisal (PRA) and Rapid Rural Appraisal (RRA). The core principles of RA include speed, field-based work, direct learning from local inhabitants, a semi-structured and multidisciplinary approach, and an emphasis on producing timely insights rather than definitive answers. RA is particularly valuable in socio-economically deprived communities where conventional methods might be too slow or resource-intensive. By rapidly gathering and analyzing information, RA helps practitioners understand community conditions and priorities, allowing for responsive and adaptive planning.

Service audits are another critical technique in community planning. This process involves systematically reviewing existing services to identify gaps, redundancies, and areas for improvement. Service audits provide a comprehensive picture of the availability and utilization of services within a community. This technique is essential for pinpointing unmet needs, optimizing resource allocation, and enhancing service delivery, ensuring that community initiatives are effectively addressing real gaps.

The Delphi technique is a structured method for gathering expert opinions and achieving consensus on complex issues. Developed by Hasson et al. (2000)[96], the Delphi technique involves several steps: selecting a panel of experts, developing and distributing an initial questionnaire, collecting and analyzing responses, and conducting iterative rounds of follow-up surveys. This process helps refine expert opinions, identify consensus, and develop informed recommendations. The Delphi technique is particularly useful in

---

96 Ibid 95

situations where diverse perspectives and expert insights are needed to address complex community issues and develop strategic plans.

In addition to these techniques, the chapter also emphasizes the importance of building a community health profile. This involves collecting and analyzing data on various health indicators to understand community health status and needs. By integrating demographic and status information, community profiles enable practitioners to identify priorities, develop targeted strategies, monitor progress, facilitate collaboration, and advocate for resources.

Overall, these techniques—Rapid Appraisal, service audits, the Delphi technique, and community health profiles—are integral to effective community planning. They provide valuable insights, enhance decision-making, and support the development of responsive and strategic initiatives to address community needs and promote overall well-being.

CHAPTER 10

LEADING WITH SPIRIT – ENERGY, LEADERSHIP AND EMPOWERMENT

Introduction

Community leadership plays a pivotal role in steering the direction of community development efforts, shaping how communities address their needs and aspirations. This chapter explores the multifaceted aspects of community leadership, focusing on its importance, the pace of development, essential competencies, and the interplay between theory and practice.

This chapter will:
- Importance in understanding community leadership: Effective community leadership is crucial for guiding and inspiring collective efforts toward achieving community goals. Leaders in community settings are responsible for mobilizing resources, fostering collaboration, and creating a shared vision for development. Their ability to engage with diverse stakeholders and

navigate complex dynamics directly impacts the success of community initiatives.

- Significance of the pace of development: The speed at which community development occurs can significantly influence the effectiveness of interventions and the community's overall progress. Understanding the factors that affect the pace of development, including resource availability, stakeholder engagement, and external pressures, helps leaders manage expectations and adapt strategies to meet evolving needs.
- Elaborate the competencies: Successful community leaders must possess a range of competencies to effectively drive development. These include strategic vision, interpersonal skills, cultural competence, and the ability to manage and resolve conflicts. Competencies also extend to understanding community dynamics, building partnerships, and leveraging data for informed decision-making.
- The application of practice, theory: The integration of theoretical frameworks with practical experience is essential for effective community leadership. This chapter examines how theoretical concepts in community development translate into actionable strategies and practices. By bridging theory and application, leaders can develop evidence-based approaches that are grounded in real-world experiences and tailored to the unique needs of their communities.

10.1. Introduction

Creating a vibrant and active community involves more than just organizing events and initiatives; it requires addressing several key challenges that can impede community engagement and sustainability. One of the foremost concerns raised by community workers is the issue of burnout among those who are dedicated to the cause. Many individuals involved in community activities often feel exhausted, experiencing what is commonly referred to as "burnout." This exhaustion is not merely physical but also emotional and psychological, arising from the constant demands and pressures associated with community work. The intense commitment required can lead to feelings of depletion, reducing one's capacity to effectively contribute and often leading to high turnover rates among volunteers and staff.

Another significant challenge is the issue of limited participation. Frequently, the same group of individuals is involved in community activities, while engaging a broader segment of the community proves to be difficult. This repetitive involvement can result in a sense of fatigue among those who are overextended and can also perpetuate a cycle where only a small fraction of the community is actively engaged. The difficulty in attracting and involving new members stems from various factors, including a lack of awareness, competing priorities, or simply a lack of interest in current offerings. Without a diverse and active base of participants, community activities can become stagnant, and the potential for fresh ideas and energy is diminished.

Compounding these issues is the pervasive sense of frustration and weariness that can pervade a community. When communities experience prolonged periods of challenge or stagnation, it can lead to a collective sense of tiredness and disillusionment. This state of fatigue makes it increasingly difficult to maintain enthusiasm and to attract and retain new members. The repetitive nature of community struggles can create a cycle where the same issues resurface, further eroding motivation and engagement.

Addressing these challenges requires a multifaceted approach. First and foremost, it's essential to recognize and mitigate burnout among community workers. This can be achieved by implementing supportive measures such as regular breaks, professional development opportunities, and adequate recognition for their efforts. Creating a supportive environment where individuals feel valued and appreciated can help alleviate some of the stress associated with community work.

Efforts to broaden community involvement should focus on diversifying engagement strategies. This might include introducing new types of activities, leveraging digital platforms to reach a wider audience, or creating opportunities for different types of contributions that cater to various interests and skills. Engaging with community members to understand their needs and preferences can help tailor activities that are more likely to attract and retain participants.

Finally, revitalizing a tired community requires a renewed focus on vision and purpose. Leaders and practitioners should work to reconnect with the community's core values and goals, fostering a sense of collective identity and shared objectives. By infusing new energy into the community's initiatives and celebrating small successes, it is possible to rebuild enthusiasm and drive positive change.

In summary, fostering a more spirited community involves

Figure 20 - Expertise in integration and implementation

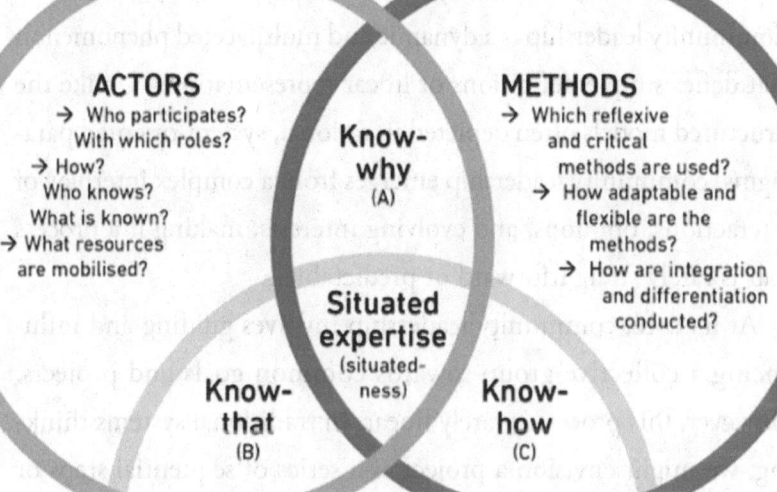

addressing issues of burnout among workers, expanding participation beyond the usual group, and overcoming general community fatigue. By focusing on these areas and implementing thoughtful, responsive strategies, community leaders can enhance engagement, invigorate their efforts, and build a more dynamic and resilient community.

10.2. Community leadership

Community leadership is a dynamic and multifaceted phenomenon that defies simple definitions or linear representations. Unlike the structured models often depicted in rational, system-oriented paradigms, community leadership emerges from a complex interplay of interactions, opinions, and evolving interests, making it a process that is rarely straightforward or predictable.

At its core, community leadership involves guiding and influencing a collective group towards common goals and projects. However, this process is rarely linear. In traditional systems thinking, we might envision a project as a series of sequential steps or a flow chart with clear cause-and-effect relationships. In contrast, community leadership operates within a web of social interactions and varying stakeholder interests, where outcomes are not always directly attributable to any single leader or action.

In the realm of community leadership, the pathways to achieving project goals are often convoluted and shaped by a multitude of factors. Leaders engage with community members, navigate differing opinions, and facilitate the formation of coalitions. This interactive and often contentious process does not lend itself to neat, predictable outcomes. Rather than having a clear, linear trajectory, community leadership involves negotiation, compromise, and continual adjustment as the community's needs and priorities evolve.

A critical aspect of community leadership is the nature of influence and impact. Unlike traditional leadership models where the leader's effect on outcomes might be more directly observable, community leadership often lacks such clear-cut visibility. The influence of a leader can be diffuse, emerging through the collective efforts of various individuals and groups rather than through any single action or decision. This can make it challenging to pinpoint the precise impact of a leader or to identify who the true leader is in any given situation.

Figure 21 - Community leadership

- Civic Leadership
- Community Leadership
- Community Engagement
- Collective Leadership

Furthermore, leadership in communities is often characterized by a lack of formal authority and the necessity of building consensus among diverse stakeholders. Leaders may emerge from within the community based on their ability to inspire, mobilize, and coordinate efforts rather than through appointed positions or official titles. The informal and fluid nature of leadership means that it can be difficult to attribute success or failure to any one individual or strategy.

Community leadership is also a process of change and adaptation. Leaders must navigate through uncertainty and resistance, fostering an environment where new ideas and approaches can take root. This ongoing process of negotiation and adjustment requires leaders to be adaptable, empathetic, and skilled in managing complex social dynamics. Success in community leadership often involves the gradual and sometimes subtle shaping of community norms, values, and actions rather than achieving immediate or visible results.

Community leadership is an intricate process marked by its non-linearity and complexity. It involves guiding a community through a fluid and interactive process of change, where influence is distributed across many individuals and outcomes are shaped by a myriad of factors. Understanding this complexity helps in recognizing that effective community leadership is not about following a fixed path but about navigating through the diverse and evolving landscape of community needs and aspirations.

10.3. The pace of development

In community development, the pace of progress is a critical factor that demands patience and respect for the natural rhythm of growth. It is essential to understand that the development process cannot be hurried without risking its overall effectiveness and sustainability. Rushing the process is a common challenge for community workers, who may feel pressured to achieve quick results. However, it is crucial to recognize that the development process belongs to the community, not the individual worker. Therefore, it must proceed according to the community's own pace, which may not align with the worker's expectations or timelines.

This principle aligns with the concept of 'organic development,' which emphasizes that change should occur gradually and through a multi-dimensional process rather than through abrupt, imposed alterations. The role of the community worker is to facilitate the right conditions for development and to assist in securing necessary resources. However, the rate at which the community evolves is largely beyond their direct control.

To illustrate this, consider the analogy of a growing plant. A plant that is forced to grow too quickly is likely to develop a weaker root system and more fragile branches, which makes it less resilient. Similarly, a community that undergoes rapid, 'quick-fix' changes is less likely to build a strong and enduring foundation. For community development to be truly successful, it must be approached as a long-term process of organic growth, where the pace of development is allowed to unfold naturally and cannot be expedited without compromising its integrity.

The relational approach to community leadership

Leadership, as conceptualized by Rost (1993)[97], is fundamentally an influence relationship between leaders and their collaborators,

---

[97] Rost, J. (1993). 'Leadership in the new millennium', *The Journal of Leadership Studies*, Vol. 1, no. 1, pp. 92-110

with a shared aim of achieving meaningful change that reflects their mutual goals. This influence is rooted in a culture of trust and hinges on the collaborative efforts of both leaders and followers. It is not merely about the actions taken by leaders towards their followers but is characterized by a process of reciprocal influence (Pigg, 1999)[98].

Relational leadership, therefore, emphasizes the significance of interactions and the process of influence that occurs between leaders and their constituents. Unlike traditional views of leadership that focus on formal positions, authority, or specific skill sets and behaviors, relational leadership is more concerned with the dynamic and interactive nature of leadership. It highlights the importance of building and nurturing relationships to bring people together with a shared sense of purpose.

When applied to community leadership, this understanding implies that the leader's role is to foster relationships within the community, whether it is a community of place or interest, to unite people around a common goal. This common purpose should always be aligned with the benefits and needs of the community. Effective community leadership thus revolves around cultivating trust and facilitating collaborative efforts to address communal issues and achieve collective objectives.

10.4. Competencies
Community leadership skills

Community leadership skills remain consistent across diverse settings, whether in communities of place or interest, and are

---

[98] Pigg, K. (1999). 'Community Leadership and community theory: A practical synthesis, *Journal of the Community Development Society,* Vol. 30, no. 2, pp. 196-212

applicable across various aspects of community development. These skills encompass a range of activities and responsibilities, including using influence to shape local programs, guiding participant activities, and actively engaging in hands-on efforts to achieve community goals, as noted by Israel and Beaulieu (1990)[99].

What truly defines effective community leadership is not the specific activities undertaken but the underlying purpose of these activities. In the realm of health and social care development, leadership is crucial in three primary areas. First, leaders must be adept at generating a shared sense of purpose or common interest around which community activities can coalesce. This involves clarifying and promoting a vision that aligns with the needs and goals of the community.

Second, leaders need to excel at bringing together different groups within the community to build a cohesive community field. This means fostering collaboration among diverse stakeholders, creating opportunities for dialogue, and integrating various perspectives to enhance collective efforts.

Third, balancing task achievement with group maintenance functions is essential. Effective leaders must ensure that while objectives are pursued, the group's dynamics and relationships are nurtured and maintained. This balance is critical for sustaining long-term engagement and ensuring that the community remains united and motivated towards its goals.

---

[99] Israel, G., Beaulieu, L. (1990) 'Community Leadership', in A.E. Luloff & L.E. Swanson (eds), *American Rural Communities*, Westview Press, Boulder, Colorado, pp. 181-202

Creating a common purpose

In community development, leadership skills are fundamental to fostering effective and meaningful progress. One key aspect of community leadership involves creating a common purpose. This requires the leader to articulate a clear and compelling vision that resonates with the collective aspirations of the community. By establishing a shared goal or objective, leaders help to unify individuals and groups, directing their efforts towards a common aim. This common purpose serves as a focal point around which community activities and initiatives can revolve, ensuring that everyone is working towards a mutually agreed-upon outcome.

Aligning personal interests with community interests is another crucial leadership skill. Effective leaders understand the importance of integrating their own goals and passions with the broader needs and aspirations of the community. This alignment ensures that personal motivations do not overshadow the community's objectives but rather complement and enhance them. Leaders who manage to harmonize their personal interests with those of the community are better positioned to inspire others, foster engagement, and build trust.

Additionally, developing a community field is an essential leadership function. This involves creating a collaborative environment where diverse groups and individuals can come together to share ideas, resources, and expertise. Leaders play a vital role in facilitating interactions among various stakeholders, fostering relationships, and nurturing a sense of collective identity. By cultivating this community field, leaders help to build a supportive network that strengthens the community's capacity to address its challenges and achieve its goals.

In summary, effective community leadership encompasses creating a unifying purpose, aligning personal and community interests, and developing a collaborative environment. These skills are integral to driving community development and ensuring that efforts are both cohesive and impactful.

Including minority groups

Community leadership is an inclusive process that must address the needs and contributions of all community members, including minority groups. Effective community leaders recognize the importance of engaging diverse populations and ensuring that all voices are heard and valued. This approach is essential for fostering a truly representative and cohesive community.

One fundamental aspect of community leadership involving minority groups is the commitment to inclusivity and equity. Leaders must actively work to dismantle barriers that may prevent minority groups from participating fully in community activities and decision-making processes. This requires understanding the unique challenges and perspectives of these groups and creating opportunities for their meaningful involvement. By ensuring that minority groups are not sidelined but rather are integral to the community's development efforts, leaders can help to promote fairness and equal representation.

Furthermore, community leaders should strive to build strong relationships with minority groups. This involves engaging in open dialogues, listening to their concerns, and acknowledging their contributions. Building trust and fostering collaboration with these groups can help to address issues of marginalization and ensure that their needs are adequately addressed in community planning and implementation. Leaders should also seek to empower minority groups by supporting their leadership development and providing platforms for their voices to be amplified within the community.

Additionally, effective community leadership involves advocating for policies and practices that support the inclusion of minority groups. Leaders should work towards creating an environment where diversity is celebrated and where systemic inequalities are actively challenged. This can involve promoting cultural competence within community organizations, developing programs that address the specific needs of minority groups, and ensuring that resources are allocated in a way that supports equitable development across all segments of the community.

Community leadership that includes minority groups requires a dedication to inclusivity, relationship-building, and advocacy. By addressing the unique needs of these groups and ensuring their active participation, leaders can foster a more equitable and cohesive community. This approach not only enhances the effectiveness of community development efforts but also strengthens the community as a whole by ensuring that all members have the opportunity to contribute to and benefit from collective progress.

10.5. Practice, theory and application

Community leadership is a multifaceted field that integrates practice, theory, and application to foster effective development and collective well-being. As a community development practitioner, understanding how these elements interplay is crucial for successful leadership and impactful community engagement.

Practice in community leadership involves the day-to-day actions and decisions that shape how a community develops. This includes building relationships, facilitating collaboration, and guiding initiatives that address local needs. Effective practice requires a deep understanding of the community's context, including its strengths, challenges, and the diversity of its members. Leaders must be adept at mobilizing resources, managing conflicts, and fostering an environment where all members can contribute to and benefit from community activities. Practical leadership involves not only strategic planning and implementation but also the ability to adapt to evolving circumstances and respond to emerging issues with flexibility and innovation.

Theory provides the foundational concepts and frameworks that inform community leadership practice. Theoretical perspectives offer insights into the dynamics of leadership, the processes of community development, and the principles of effective engagement. For instance, theories of relational leadership emphasize the importance of interactions and mutual influence between leaders and community members. These theories highlight that leadership is not solely about positional authority but about fostering trust, collaboration, and shared purpose. Other theoretical frameworks, such as participatory and asset-based community development, focus on involving community members in the decision-making process and leveraging local strengths to drive progress. Understanding these theories helps leaders to apply best practices and adapt strategies based on proven principles.

Application refers to how theoretical concepts are put into practice within specific community contexts. This involves translating theoretical knowledge into actionable strategies that address the unique needs and goals of the community. For example, a leader might apply theories of participatory development by organizing community forums to solicit input and build consensus on local projects. Similarly, applying asset-based development principles could involve identifying and mobilizing existing community resources and strengths to achieve developmental goals. Effective application requires not only theoretical knowledge but also practical skills in project management, facilitation, and negotiation. Leaders must be able to assess the needs of their communities, design appropriate interventions, and evaluate the outcomes to ensure that strategies are effective and aligned with the community's evolving needs.

In summary, community leadership is an integrated approach that combines practice, theory, and application. Understanding and effectively implementing these components allows leaders to foster meaningful community engagement, drive development efforts, and achieve sustainable outcomes. By grounding their actions in theoretical knowledge and adapting strategies to real-world contexts, community leaders can enhance their effectiveness and contribute positively to the communities they serve.

10.6 Summary

Community leadership is fundamentally a multidimensional process that involves a dynamic interplay of interactions among community members. This perspective emphasizes that leadership in a community context is not solely about holding a formal position or title, but rather about the influence exerted by individuals who are able to inspire and guide others. Unlike organizational leadership, which is often defined by formal roles and hierarchical structures, community leadership relies on the ability to mobilize people and build consensus through collaboration and shared purpose.

A critical aspect of community leadership is identifying and articulating a common purpose that resonates with diverse groups within the community. This common purpose serves as the foundation for collective action and helps to unite individuals across different sectors, interest groups, and cultural backgrounds. The challenge lies in bringing these varied groups together and fostering a sense of shared commitment to the community's goals.

One of the key challenges in community leadership is ensuring that leadership responsibilities are distributed effectively across different interest groups. Often, a small number of individuals may end up taking on multiple roles, which can lead to burnout and inefficiency. Therefore, a significant leadership task is to harness and direct the energy and enthusiasm of community members in a way that is both productive and sustainable. This involves recognizing and supporting emerging leaders and ensuring that leadership responsibilities are appropriately shared.

Sustainability of community leadership is another crucial consideration. To maintain momentum and engagement, it is important to regularly organize activities that bring community members together to reflect on leadership issues and assess progress. These reflective activities help to reinforce the common purpose, address any emerging challenges, and ensure that leadership efforts remain aligned with the community's evolving needs and aspirations.

In summary, community leadership is a complex process that hinges on influence, shared purpose, and effective collaboration. It requires leaders to mobilize diverse groups, manage leadership distribution, and foster sustainability through regular reflection and engagement activities. By addressing these aspects, community leaders can enhance their effectiveness and contribute to the long-term success and cohesion of their communities.

PART FOUR

BUILDING KNOWLEDGE, SKILLS AND OTHER COMPETENCIES

In the realm of community development, the cultivation of knowledge, skills, and competencies is essential for fostering effective and sustainable progress. Part 04 of this guide delves into the multifaceted nature of building these essential attributes, focusing on a holistic approach to developing the competencies required for successful community leadership and facilitation.

Chapter 11, titled "Holistic Approach in Competencies," sets the stage by exploring the comprehensive skill set necessary for effective community development. This chapter begins by introducing the concept of a holistic approach to competencies, which integrates various skills and values crucial for navigating the complex landscape of community work. It emphasizes the importance of a well-rounded skill set that encompasses not only technical and procedural knowledge but also interpersonal and ethical considerations.

The chapter then moves on to detail specific community facilitative skills, which are vital for guiding and supporting community groups through collaborative processes and decision-making. These skills enable leaders to effectively manage group dynamics, mediate conflicts, and foster productive dialogue among diverse stakeholders.

In addition, the chapter addresses community representation skills, which involve advocating for the needs and interests of different community segments, ensuring that all voices are heard, and that diverse perspectives are represented in decision-making processes. This aspect of community leadership is crucial for maintaining inclusivity and equity.

The discussion continues with an exploration of community development skills, which cover the strategic planning and implementation of initiatives that address community needs and promote sustainable growth. These skills are essential for translating community goals into actionable plans and effective outcomes.

Moreover, Chapter 11 highlights the significance of understanding community values and ethics. Leaders must be attuned to the cultural norms and ethical standards of the communities they serve, ensuring that their actions align with the community's values and foster trust and respect.

Creating support networks is also a key focus, as building connections and partnerships within and outside the community enhances the capacity for collective action and resource mobilization. Effective leaders must be adept at establishing and nurturing these networks to support community development efforts.

Finally, Chapter 11 concludes with a summary that reinforces the interconnectedness of these competencies and their collective impact on community development.

Chapter 12 shifts the focus to "Helpful Resources," offering an introduction to various tools and resources available to community development practitioners. This chapter provides valuable information on free courses, online resources, and other materials that can aid in skill development and knowledge enhancement. By highlighting these resources, Chapter 12 aims to equip practitioners with additional support for their continuous learning and professional growth.

In conclusion, Part 04 of this guide provides a comprehensive overview of the competencies required for effective community leadership, emphasizing the importance of a holistic approach to skill development and resource utilization. This section serves as a foundational resource for practitioners seeking to enhance their capabilities and contribute to meaningful and sustainable community development.

CHAPTER 11

HOLISTIC APPROACH IN COMPETENCIES

Introduction

This chapter will:
- Importance in understanding the holistic approach in competencies
- Significance of different skills sets that complement the community development process

11.1. Introduction

Chapter 11 of this guide, titled "Holistic Approach in Competencies," introduces a comprehensive framework for understanding and developing the multifaceted skills necessary for effective community development. This chapter explores a holistic approach to competencies, highlighting how a diverse set of skills and attributes come together to drive successful community leadership and facilitation.

The chapter begins by outlining the importance of a holistic perspective, emphasizing that community development requires more than just technical expertise. It involves a nuanced understanding of various competencies that interact and complement each other to foster meaningful progress within communities.

It then delves into community facilitative skills, which are essential for guiding groups through collaborative processes and facilitating productive interactions. These skills include managing group dynamics, mediating conflicts, and fostering inclusive dialogue, all of which are crucial for effective community engagement and decision-making.

Following this, the chapter addresses community representation skills, which are vital for ensuring that the needs and perspectives of diverse community segments are accurately represented and advocated for. Effective community leaders must be adept at balancing multiple viewpoints and ensuring that all voices are heard in the decision-making process.

The discussion then moves to community development skills, focusing on the strategic planning and implementation required to address community needs and promote sustainable growth. This includes the ability to translate community goals into actionable plans and successfully execute initiatives that drive positive outcomes.

Additionally, Chapter 11 covers community values and ethics, underscoring the importance of aligning leadership practices with the cultural norms and ethical standards of the community. Understanding and respecting these values is essential for building trust and maintaining effective relationships with community members.

The chapter also highlights the role of creating support networks, which involves establishing and nurturing connections both within and outside the community. Strong support networks enhance the capacity for collective action and resource mobilization, further supporting community development efforts.

The chapter concludes with a summary that reinforces the interconnected nature of these competencies and their collective impact on community development. It reiterates the importance of a holistic approach in cultivating the skills necessary for effective leadership and sustainable progress.

11.2. Community facilitative roles and skills

In the field of community development, the facilitative roles and skills of community workers are crucial for stimulating and supporting the growth and progress of communities. These roles involve more than just administrative or managerial tasks; they are deeply engaged in fostering an environment where community members can come together to address their needs, collaborate on solutions, and drive meaningful change.

At the heart of facilitative roles is the ability to act as a catalyst for action. Community workers use a variety of techniques to encourage and guide community processes, helping to mobilize individuals and groups towards collective goals. This catalytic role is essential for igniting community engagement and sustaining momentum throughout development initiatives.

Within the broader category of facilitative roles, several specific functions can be identified. Social animation is one such role, where community workers energize and motivate individuals, creating an atmosphere conducive to active participation and collaboration. This involves fostering enthusiasm and commitment among community members, which is critical for building a vibrant and engaged community.

Mediation and negotiation are also key components of facilitative roles. Community workers often find themselves navigating conflicts and differing perspectives within the community. By mediating disputes and negotiating solutions, they help to maintain harmony and ensure that diverse viewpoints are considered in the decision-making process. This role is vital for creating an inclusive environment where all voices can be heard and respected.

Support is another crucial aspect of facilitative roles. Community workers provide various forms of support, including emotional encouragement, practical assistance, and resources to help individuals and groups achieve their goals. This support is essential for empowering community members and reinforcing their capacity to contribute effectively to community development.

Building consensus is a specific role within facilitation that focuses on achieving agreement among community members. By guiding discussions and facilitating collaborative decision-making processes, community workers help to align different interests and perspectives towards a common purpose. This role is critical for ensuring that community initiatives are supported by a broad base of stakeholders.

Group facilitation is also a key component of facilitative roles. Community workers lead and manage group interactions, ensuring that meetings and discussions are productive and focused. Effective group facilitation involves structuring conversations, managing group dynamics, and encouraging active participation from all members.

Utilization of skills and resources is another important aspect. Community workers identify and leverage the existing skills and resources within the community to enhance development efforts.

Figure 22 -Community workpractice roles

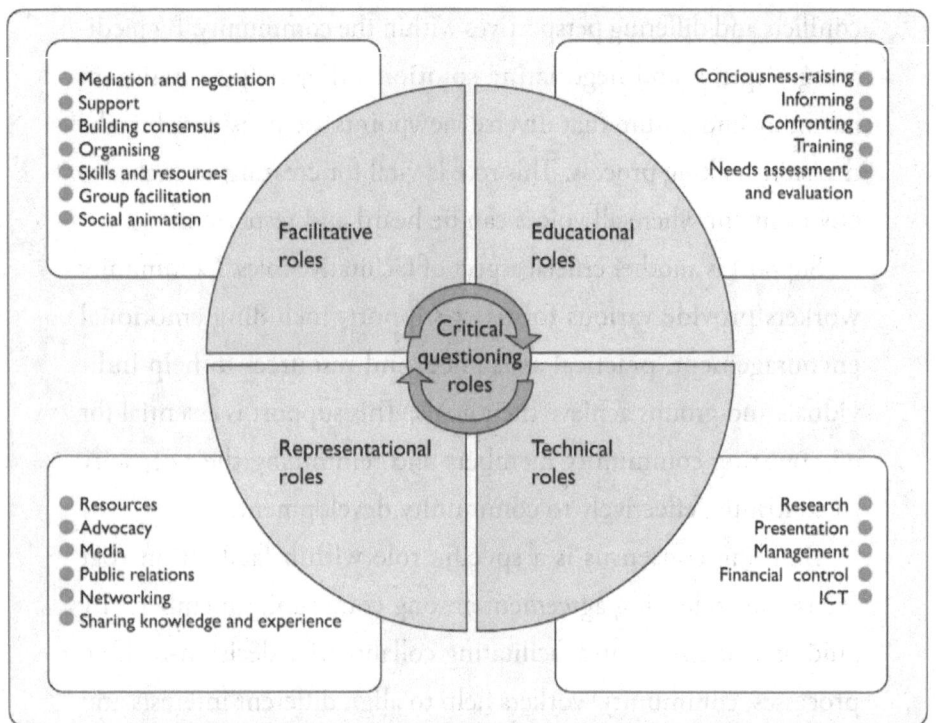

By effectively utilizing these assets, they maximize the potential for success and sustainability of community initiatives.

Organizing is a practical role that involves coordinating activities, events, and programs within the community. Community workers are responsible for planning and implementing various initiatives, ensuring that they are executed efficiently and effectively. This role requires strong organizational skills and the ability to manage multiple tasks and priorities.

In summary, facilitative roles in community development encompass a range of functions aimed at stimulating, supporting, and guiding community growth. By employing techniques such as social animation, mediation, negotiation, support, consensus building, group facilitation, resource utilization, and organizing, community workers play a pivotal role in driving positive change and fostering a collaborative and engaged community.

11.3. Community representational roles and skills

In the field of community development, community representational roles and skills are essential for effectively interfacing with external bodies on behalf of the community. These roles involve engaging with a broader system beyond the immediate community to secure resources, advocate for community needs, and promote the community's interests. While much of a community worker's activities are concentrated within the community, the ability to navigate and interact with external entities is crucial for achieving comprehensive and sustainable development.

One of the primary representational roles is obtaining resources. Community workers often need to secure funding, materials, or other resources from external sources such as government agencies, non-profit organizations, or private sector partners. This involves identifying potential resource providers, preparing proposals or applications, and negotiating terms that align with the community's needs and goals. Effective resource acquisition requires not only an understanding of the community's requirements but also the ability to articulate these needs convincingly to external stakeholders.

Advocacy is another critical representational role. Community workers act as champions for the community's interests, striving to influence policy decisions, secure support for community projects, and address systemic issues that affect the community. Advocacy involves understanding the broader policy environment, engaging with policymakers, and mobilizing community members to support advocacy efforts. It requires a strategic approach to ensure that the community's voice is heard and considered in decision-making processes that impact its well-being.

Using the media is a valuable skill in representational roles. Community workers leverage various media platforms to raise awareness about community issues, promote initiatives, and highlight successes. Effective use of the media involves crafting compelling messages, utilizing different communication channels, and engaging with journalists or media outlets to ensure that the community's story is shared widely. This role is crucial for building public support, informing stakeholders, and enhancing the community's visibility.

Public relations and public presentation are also integral to representational roles. Community workers often engage in activities that shape the public perception of the community and its initiatives. This includes managing relationships with external stakeholders, organizing events or presentations, and maintaining a positive image of the community. Strong public relations skills help in fostering goodwill, establishing partnerships, and ensuring that the community's efforts are recognized and valued by external audiences.

Sharing knowledge and experience is another essential aspect of representational roles. Community workers have valuable insights and expertise gained from working within the community. By sharing this knowledge with external organizations, peers, or other communities, they contribute to the broader field of community development. This sharing of experiences not only benefits others but also helps to build networks of support and collaboration that can further enhance community development efforts.

In summary, community representational roles are pivotal for connecting the community with external entities and advancing its interests. These roles encompass obtaining resources, advocating for needs, utilizing the media, managing public relations, and sharing knowledge. By effectively performing these representational functions, community workers play a crucial role in bridging the gap between the community and the wider system, ensuring that the community's needs are addressed, and its contributions are recognized.

11.4. Community development skills
In community work, skills are not simply acquired through rote memorization or standardized training manuals. Unlike technical or procedural knowledge that can be systematically taught and assessed, the skills required for effective community work are deeply rooted in personal experience, continuous reflection, and adaptive learning. While practice manuals and classroom instruction serve as valuable resources, they only lay the groundwork for a journey that each community worker must undertake on their own. The essence of mastering community work lies not in the static acquisition of skills but in their dynamic development—a process that is as much about personal growth as it is about professional competence.

Community work is inherently unpredictable and varied. Unlike fields that follow rigid, formulaic approaches, community work demands a fluidity of thought and action. It requires workers to navigate diverse and often complex social landscapes, adapt to evolving circumstances, and engage with a wide array of individuals and groups. This ever-changing environment means that community work is more of an art than a science. The worker's path is not a straight line but a meandering journey that defies predictable outcomes.

In light of this, the development of community work skills is a highly individualized process. Rather than being handed a set of skills through a traditional educational framework, community workers must define and cultivate their own abilities. This development is not solely the responsibility of teachers, trainers, or supervisors. Instead, it is incumbent upon the workers themselves to engage deeply with their practice and continuously refine their skills.

Central to this developmental process are five key components: analysis, awareness, learning from others, and intuition. Each of these elements plays a crucial role in helping community workers forge their unique set of skills and approaches.

Analysis involves a critical examination of the community context, the needs of its members, and the effectiveness of different interventions. Community workers must assess their own practices, the outcomes they achieve, and the dynamics at play within the communities they serve. This ongoing analysis helps workers understand what strategies are successful and why, and it informs future actions and decisions.

Awareness encompasses both self-awareness and situational awareness. Community workers must be attuned to their own strengths, weaknesses, biases, and emotional responses. This self-awareness allows them to manage their own reactions and interactions more effectively. At the same time, awareness of the community's needs, values, and cultural nuances is essential for delivering relevant and respectful support.

Learning from others is an integral part of skill development.

Community workers benefit from observing and engaging with peers, mentors, and other professionals. By sharing experiences and insights, they gain new perspectives and strategies that can enhance their own practice. This collaborative learning process fosters a richer understanding of different approaches and solutions.

Intuition is perhaps the most elusive but equally important aspect of skill development. It involves the ability to make informed decisions and take actions based on an intrinsic sense of what feels right or appropriate in a given situation. Intuition is honed through experience and reflection, allowing community workers to respond to complex and unpredictable scenarios with creativity and insight.

Together, these components contribute to a broader openness to learning and a commitment to reflective practice. Openness to learning means being receptive to new ideas, willing to experiment with different approaches, and ready to adapt based on feedback and results. Reflective practice involves regularly evaluating one's own work, considering how one's actions impact others, and seeking continuous improvement.

In a nutshell, the development of community work skills is a deeply personal and evolving process. It is not about mastering a fixed set of techniques but rather about engaging in a continuous journey of growth and adaptation. Community workers must navigate this journey with a blend of analysis, awareness, learning from others, and intuition. By embracing these components and remaining committed to reflective practice, they can cultivate a unique and effective set of skills that meets the needs of the communities they serve.

11.5. Community values and ethics

Community work, by its very essence, transcends the boundaries of mere technical proficiency. It is deeply embedded in a tapestry of values and ethical considerations that shape its practice. The nature of community work inherently involves a set of values, such as the value of community itself, democracy, participation, and self-determination. These values are not only implicit but also explicit in the practice of community work, guiding its principles and methodologies. This chapter delves into the intricate relationship between community values, ethics, and the practice of community work, highlighting how personal and moral values intersect with professional responsibilities.

At its core, community work is an expression of communal values. It is grounded in the belief that communities have the power and right to shape their own destinies, to participate actively in decisions that affect their lives, and to exercise self-determination. These values are crucial, as they underpin the very framework of community development. Earlier chapters of this book have outlined these values within the context of ecological sustainability and social justice/human rights, establishing a solid foundation for understanding the ethical dimensions of community work.

However, the practice of community work cannot be divorced from personal values. Every community worker brings to their role a unique set of personal beliefs and values. These personal values, which may be shaped by cultural, religious, or philosophical influences, interact with the values inherent in community work. The interplay between these personal values and professional values can sometimes lead to significant conflicts. For instance, consider a scenario where a community worker's personal perspective on gender fluidity clashes with the traditional views of a community they are serving. This conflict can lead to friction, potentially undermining the effectiveness of the community worker's efforts.

The resolution of such conflicts is not always straightforward. When personal values clash with the values of the community or those of fellow workers, it can create substantial challenges. Effective management of these conflicts involves a deep self-awareness and a commitment to critically reflective practice. Community workers must recognize their own values and understand how these values might impact their work. They must also be prepared to navigate and address conflicts in a manner that respects the diverse values within the community and among their colleagues.

In addition to personal value conflicts, community workers often face moral and ethical dilemmas. These dilemmas arise when workers must make decisions that involve conflicting moral principles or ethical standards. Although there is no universal code of ethics for community workers—unless they are affiliated with a specific profession such as social work, law, or psychology—certain ethical principles are implied in the practice of community work. These principles guide workers in making sound moral judgments and navigating complex situations.

Ethical dilemmas in community work can be categorized into four broad areas:

1. **Conflict with Community:** Community workers may encounter situations where their professional responsibilities or personal values conflict with the values or expectations of the community they are serving. For example, a worker might face challenges in promoting community development initiatives that are at odds with the traditional norms of a local community. Navigating

these conflicts requires sensitivity, diplomacy, and a deep understanding of the community's values and needs.

2. **Conflict with Employers or Funding Bodies:** Community workers often operate within frameworks established by their employers or funding agencies. These frameworks can sometimes impose constraints that may not align with the worker's professional judgment or the needs of the community. Workers might face ethical dilemmas when their professional responsibilities conflict with the directives or expectations of these entities. Managing such conflicts involves negotiation, advocacy, and a clear understanding of the ethical implications of various funding conditions or organizational policies.

3. **Issues of Information and Communication:** The ethical management of information is crucial in community work. Workers must handle sensitive information with care, ensuring confidentiality and integrity in their communication. Dilemmas arise when there is pressure to disclose confidential information or when transparency is compromised. Upholding ethical standards in information management requires a commitment to honesty, respect for privacy, and adherence to professional guidelines.

4. **Laws and Regulations:** Community workers must navigate a landscape of legal and regulatory requirements. These laws can sometimes conflict with the ethical principles of community work or the needs of the community. For instance, legal obligations regarding reporting or compliance might come into tension with the worker's commitment to community values or ethical standards. Workers must balance legal responsibilities with ethical considerations, often requiring nuanced

judgment and a thorough understanding of both legal and ethical frameworks.

In context, Community work is a complex field where values and ethics play a fundamental role. The interaction between personal values, community values, and professional ethics creates a dynamic landscape that community workers must navigate with care and sensitivity. By embracing a critically reflective approach, understanding the sources of value conflicts, and addressing ethical dilemmas thoughtfully, community workers can uphold the integrity of their practice and contribute effectively to the communities they serve.

11.6. Creating support networks

Community work, despite its inherent challenges, need not be a solitary endeavor. The notion of the community worker as a lone figure, grappling with the demands of their role in isolation, runs counter to the fundamental principles of community work. This field is, by its very nature, a collective and social endeavor. Far from being a solitary struggle, community work is enriched by a tapestry of relationships and networks that provide crucial support and shared learning.

The image of the isolated community worker, battling through difficulties alone, is often a misconception. It reflects a misunderstanding of the collaborative essence that defines community work. In reality, community work thrives on collective engagement and mutual support. The true challenge for many community workers is not the solitude of their role but rather the difficulty in finding time for personal reflection and self-care amidst the demands of their work.

To navigate the complexities of community work and maintain

personal well-being, community workers need to cultivate a range of support systems. These sources of support are not just beneficial but essential for making sense of the job and ensuring personal resilience. Here are the key avenues through which community workers can find the support they need:

Firstly, employers play a critical role in providing support. A supportive employer understands the demands of community work and offers a framework that enables workers to perform effectively. This support might include resources, training opportunities, and an organizational culture that values and encourages professional development. A positive relationship with an employer can help mitigate the pressures of the job and foster a sense of belonging within the organization.

Co-workers are another vital source of support. The nature of community work often involves teamwork and collaboration. Co-workers can offer practical assistance, share insights, and provide emotional support. Building strong, supportive relationships with colleagues can create a network of mutual assistance, where workers can exchange experiences, seek advice, and offer encouragement. This collaborative environment can alleviate feelings of isolation and enhance the overall effectiveness of community work.

Workers in other communities also serve as valuable resources. Networking with community workers from different areas allows for the exchange of ideas, strategies, and experiences. This broader perspective can offer new insights and solutions to challenges faced in one's own community. Such connections foster a sense of solidarity and provide opportunities for learning from a diverse range of practices and approaches.

Community members themselves can be an important source of

support. Engaging with the very people who benefit from community work helps build trust and understanding. These relationships can provide feedback, highlight community needs, and offer a sense of purpose. By involving community members in the process, workers can gain support and validation for their efforts, as well as practical assistance and collaboration on initiatives.

Activist networks are another avenue through which community workers can find support. These networks often consist of individuals and organizations dedicated to social change and advocacy. They can offer resources, strategic guidance, and a sense of shared mission. Activist networks provide a platform for collective action and support, amplifying the impact of community work and connecting workers with broader social movements.

Lastly, personal networks are crucial for sustaining personal well-being and professional effectiveness. Friends, family, and mentors outside of the community work environment can offer emotional support, practical advice, and a necessary break from the rigors of the job. These personal connections provide a space for reflection, relaxation, and rejuvenation, helping community workers maintain balance and perspective.

In summary, community work, while challenging, does not need to be experienced in isolation. By actively seeking and engaging with various sources of support—employers, co-workers, workers in other communities, community members, activist networks, and personal connections—community workers can navigate their roles more effectively and sustain their personal well-being. The essence of community work lies in its collective nature, and embracing this aspect can transform the experience from one of solitude to one of shared purpose and mutual support.

11.7. Summary

Chapter 11 of this guide, titled "Holistic Approach in Competencies," provides an in-depth exploration of the comprehensive skills needed for effective community development, emphasizing the interconnectedness of various competencies in fostering successful community leadership. The chapter asserts that community development is not merely about technical proficiency but requires a broad array of skills that work together to promote meaningful progress.

The chapter begins by underscoring the importance of a holistic perspective in community work. It highlights that effective community development necessitates more than just technical skills; it involves a nuanced understanding of how various competencies interact and complement each other. This holistic approach is essential for driving progress within communities and ensuring that community development efforts are well-rounded and impactful.

Community facilitative skills are explored as a crucial aspect of this holistic framework. These skills are essential for guiding groups through collaborative processes and fostering productive interactions. Effective facilitation involves managing group dynamics, mediating conflicts, and encouraging inclusive dialogue. These abilities are critical for engaging community members and facilitating effective decision-making.

The chapter also addresses community representation skills, emphasizing their importance in ensuring that diverse community perspectives are accurately represented and advocated for. Community leaders must adeptly balance multiple viewpoints and ensure that all voices are heard during the decision-making process. This skill is vital for ensuring that community initiatives reflect the needs and desires of all segments of the population.

Additionally, community development skills are discussed, focusing on the strategic planning and implementation necessary to address community needs and promote sustainable growth. This involves translating community goals into actionable plans and executing initiatives that drive positive outcomes. Effective community development requires both strategic foresight and practical implementation abilities.

The chapter further examines the role of community values and ethics. It stresses that community work is intrinsically linked to values such as democracy, participation, and self-determination. These values underpin the practice of community work and guide its principles and methodologies. Personal values of community workers also play a significant role and can sometimes lead to conflicts with community or professional values. Effective management of these conflicts requires a deep understanding of both personal and community values and a commitment to reflective practice.

Creating support networks is another key theme of the chapter. Despite the challenges of community work, it need not be a solitary endeavor. Instead, community workers should seek support from various sources, including employers, co-workers, other community workers, community members, activist networks, and personal connections. Building and nurturing these support systems are essential for maintaining personal well-being and enhancing professional effectiveness.

In summary, Chapter 11 emphasizes the importance of a holistic approach to competencies in community development. It highlights the need for a diverse set of skills—ranging from facilitative and representational roles to strategic development and ethical considerations—that work together to drive successful community initiatives. By embracing these interconnected competencies and fostering strong support networks, community workers can enhance their effectiveness and contribute meaningfully to the communities they serve. The chapter underscores that community work is a collective and social endeavor, where collaboration and mutual support are pivotal for achieving sustainable progress.

CHAPTER 12

HELPFUL RESOURCES

Introduction

This chapter will:
- Serve as a guide to navigating the myriad tools and opportunities available for community workers and practitioners seeking to enhance their skills and knowledge.
- Delve into the specifics of available resources, including a variety of free courses and educational materials

12.1. Introduction

In the ever-evolving landscape of community development and professional growth, having access to the right resources can make a significant difference in one's ability to contribute effectively and adapt to new challenges. This chapter, titled "Helpful Resources," serves as a guide to navigating the myriad tools and opportunities available for community workers and practitioners seeking to enhance their skills and knowledge.

The chapter begins with a comprehensive introduction to the

value of resources in community work. Understanding and utilizing available resources is crucial for staying updated with best practices, gaining new skills, and addressing the dynamic needs of communities. This introduction sets the stage for exploring the range of resources that can support professional development and enhance the impact of community initiatives.

Following the introduction, the chapter delves into the specifics of available resources, including a variety of free courses and educational materials. The landscape of online learning and open-access resources has expanded dramatically, offering numerous opportunities for community workers to gain valuable knowledge without financial constraints. This section highlights key platforms and programs that provide free courses relevant to community development, leadership, and other essential areas. It also offers guidance on how to select and make the most of these resources to align with individual learning goals and professional needs.

The chapter then presents a summary of the resources discussed, encapsulating the key points and takeaways. This summary provides a concise overview of the available tools and educational opportunities, reinforcing their importance and utility for community workers striving for continuous improvement and effective practice.

In the conclusion, the chapter emphasizes the critical role that ongoing learning and resource utilization play in the field of community development. It reiterates that while community work can be challenging and complex, the array of resources at one's disposal can significantly ease the journey. By actively engaging with these resources, community workers can stay informed, enhance their skills, and ultimately contribute more effectively to their communities. The chapter closes with a call to action, encouraging readers to explore and leverage these resources to support their professional growth and community development efforts.

12.2. Resources and available free courses

As a community development practitioner in Australia, staying updated with the latest knowledge and skills is vital for effectively contributing to community growth[100] and transformation. Fortunately, there are numerous free resources and courses available that can enhance professional practice without imposing a financial burden. These resources are designed to support practitioners in areas such as community engagement, leadership, governance, and more.

Figure 23 - Community Development Chain

Capacity building community development process	Social capital	Community development outcome
Developing the ability to act	The ability to act	Taking action Community improvement

One valuable resource is the suite of free online courses offered through the Australian may stakeholders across the country to provide a variety of courses relevant to community development professionals.

Another significant source of free educational content is the

---

100 Phillips R and Pittman R H (2009) An Introduction to Community Development. Routledge.

Department of Social Services. The department's website offers access to several free online modules and training resources tailored to social service professionals. These modules cover essential topics such as welfare services, community engagement, and program evaluation, making them a useful tool for community development practitioners seeking to expand their knowledge and skills (Department of Social Services, 2024).

The Australian Council of Social Service (ACOSS) also provides a wealth of free resources. ACOSS focuses on social justice and community development issues, offering access to research reports, policy briefs, and educational materials that are beneficial for practitioners involved in advocacy and community support. These resources help professionals stay informed about current issues and effective strategies for addressing social challenges (ACOSS, 2024).

TAFE institutions across Australia are another excellent resource for free or low-cost training. TAFE NSW, for example, offers a range of short courses and workshops in community services, including topics such as youth work, mental health support, and community development. These courses are designed to enhance practical skills and provide up-to-date knowledge for those working in the field (TAFE NSW, 2024).

In Western Australia, the Office of Multicultural Interests offers a particularly valuable course for those interested in leadership and governance within diverse communities. The "Leadership & Governance" course is designed to equip community leaders with the skills necessary to navigate the complexities of multicultural environments. This course covers key aspects of effective leadership, including governance structures, strategic planning, and community engagement strategies, all tailored to the unique needs of multicultural communities (Office of Multicultural Interests, 2024)[101].

Additionally, the Australian Red Cross provides training resources and online courses focusing on emergency management. These resources are especially relevant for community workers involved in disaster response and recovery, offering practical skills and strategies for managing crises and supporting affected communities (Australian Red Cross, 2024).

By utilizing these free resources and courses, community development practitioners in Australia can enhance their expertise and effectiveness in their roles. These opportunities not only contribute to their professional growth but also support their capacity to drive positive change and development within their communities.

Useful resources

Department of Communities – Western Australia. Retrieved from https://www.wa.gov.au/organisation/department-of-communities

The Western Australian Council of Social Service - https://www.wacoss.org.au/

ACOSS. (2024). *Australian Council of Social Service: Publications and resources*. Retrieved from - https://www.acoss.org.au

Australian Red Cross. (2024). *Training and resources*. Retrieved from https://www.redcross.org.au/governance/reconciliation-action-plan/

Department of Social Services. (2024). *Training and resources*. Retrieved from https://www.dss.gov.au/grants

---

101 Extracted from publicly available - OMI website: https://www.omi.wa.gov.au/docs/librariesprovider

Office of Multicultural Interests, Western Australia. (2024). *Leadership & Governance course*. Retrieved from https://www.omi.wa.gov.au/resources-and-statistics/educational-resources

TAFE NSW. (2024). *Free courses in community services*. Retrieved from https://www.tafensw.edu.au/

12.3. Summary

In the field of community development, accessing the right resources is paramount for practitioners striving to enhance their skills and stay abreast of new developments. Chapter 12, titled "Helpful Resources," serves as a comprehensive guide to navigating the vast array of tools and educational opportunities available to community workers. This chapter underscores the significance of continuous professional development and the role that free resources and courses play in supporting community development efforts.

The chapter opens with an introduction to the critical importance of utilizing available resources in community work. It sets the context by highlighting how essential it is for practitioners to engage with ongoing learning and professional development. These resources not only help in updating best practices but also in adapting to the changing needs of the communities they serve. Understanding and leveraging these tools is crucial for maintaining effective practice and fostering community growth.

Following this introduction, the chapter delves into specific free resources and educational materials accessible to community development professionals. The landscape of online learning has significantly expanded, providing numerous opportunities for acquiring valuable knowledge without incurring financial costs. One prominent example is the suite of free online courses offered by various Australian stakeholders. These platforms, in collaboration with universities and educational institutions, offer a range of courses relevant to community development, leadership, and other critical areas.

The Department of Social Services (DSS) stands out as a significant source of free educational content. The DSS website provides access to a variety of online modules and training resources tailored for social service professionals. These resources cover essential topics such as welfare services, community engagement, and program evaluation. They serve as a valuable tool for community development practitioners who are keen to expand their expertise and adapt to evolving community needs (Department of Social Services, 2024).

Additionally, the Australian Council of Social Service (ACOSS) offers a wealth of resources focused on social justice and community development. ACOSS provides access to research reports, policy briefs, and educational materials that are particularly beneficial for practitioners involved in advocacy and support roles. These resources help professionals stay informed about current issues and effective strategies for addressing social challenges (ACOSS, 2024).

TAFE institutions across Australia also play a crucial role in providing free or low-cost training. For instance, TAFE NSW offers a variety of short courses and workshops in community services. Topics include youth work, mental health support, and general community development. These courses are designed to enhance practical skills and provide up-to-date knowledge essential for those working in the field (TAFE NSW, 2024).

In Western Australia, the Office of Multicultural Interests offers a particularly notable free course focused on leadership and governance within multicultural contexts. The "Leadership &

Governance" course is tailored to equip community leaders with the necessary skills to navigate the complexities of diverse communities. It covers crucial aspects of effective leadership, including governance structures, strategic planning, and community engagement strategies, addressing the unique needs of multicultural environments (Office of Multicultural Interests, 2024).

Furthermore, the Australian Red Cross provides valuable training resources and online courses centered on emergency management. These resources are especially relevant for community workers involved in disaster response and recovery, offering practical skills and strategies for managing crises and supporting affected communities (Australian Red Cross, 2024).

In summary, the chapter emphasizes that by taking advantage of these free resources and courses, community development practitioners in Australia can significantly enhance their professional capabilities. Engaging with these educational opportunities not only supports personal growth but also strengthens their ability to drive positive change within their communities. The chapter concludes with a reaffirmation of the importance of continuous learning and encourages practitioners to actively explore and utilize these valuable resources to support their ongoing development and community impact.

12.4. Conclusion

In concluding this exploration of community development and engagement, it is crucial to reflect on the wealth of information presented and its potential impact on society. This book has traversed the multifaceted landscape of community work, offering insights and practical guidance for those dedicated to fostering stronger, more resilient communities.

The journey began with a foundational understanding of what constitutes a community, delving into its definition, structural elements, and functions. By establishing a clear grasp of community dynamics, readers were equipped to appreciate the significance of community capacity and the unique strengths and social factors that contribute to it. This early groundwork set the stage for a deeper exploration of culturally and linguistically diverse (CaLD) perspectives, emphasizing the importance of understanding and working effectively with migrant communities.

The second part of the book focused on practical aspects of working with communities. It provided a thorough examination of conceptual approaches and frameworks essential for engaging with communities. From participative democracy to integrative partnerships, these frameworks offered a structured approach to building and maintaining productive community relationships. The examination of government-community partnerships further highlighted the roles and responsibilities of various stakeholders in community development, emphasizing the need for collaborative efforts to advance community services and engagement.

The subsequent chapters addressed the skills required for effective community engagement, particularly from a CaLD perspective. The discussions on community decision-making, partnerships, and planning were tailored to enhance practitioners' abilities to navigate the complexities of diverse community needs and foster inclusive decision-making processes. The exploration of community leadership and empowerment underscored the importance of energy, competency, and application in driving community development efforts.

The book then shifted focus to building the necessary knowledge, skills, and competencies for community work. It offered a holistic approach to developing facilitative, representational, and developmental skills, alongside the ethical considerations and support networks crucial for successful community engagement. This comprehensive examination was designed to equip practitioners with the tools they need to effect meaningful change and support community growth.

In the final chapter, readers were introduced to a range of free resources and courses available in Australia, including those focused on leadership and governance, community planning, and emergency management. These resources serve as invaluable tools for ongoing professional development, enabling community workers to stay informed and enhance their practice without financial constraints.

The target audience for this book encompasses community development practitioners, social service professionals, and anyone involved in community engagement and leadership. The content is tailored to meet the needs of individuals seeking to improve their understanding and effectiveness in working with diverse communities. By providing practical insights, conceptual frameworks, and access to valuable resources, this book aims to empower readers to contribute more effectively to their communities.

The anticipated impact of this book on society is profound. By equipping practitioners with a comprehensive understanding of community dynamics, practical frameworks, and essential skills, the book fosters the development of stronger, more cohesive communities. The emphasis on inclusive practices, particularly within CaLD contexts, aims to promote social justice, equity, and active participation. Ultimately, this book serves as a catalyst for positive change, enabling practitioners to build and sustain communities that are resilient, empowered, and responsive to the needs of all their members.

REFERENCES

Australian Bureau of Statistics. (2021). *Census of Population and Housing: Reflecting Australia - Stories from the Census, 2021*. Retrieved from Australian Bureau of Statistics.

Australian Bureau of Statistics. (2022). *2021 Census QuickStats*. Retrieved from Australian Bureau of Statistics.

Australian Government. (2021). *Australian Government Multicultural Policy*. Retrieved from Australian Government.

Anderson, B. (2016). *Imagined communities*. Verso Books.

Allan Johnson, Human Arrangements, Harcourt Brace Jovanovich Publishers: Orlando, 1986, p. 692).

Auspos. P, Kubisch, A. (2004) Building knowledge about community change – moving beyond evaluations. Washington: The Aspen institute Roundtable on Community Change.

Black, A. Hughes, P. (2001), *The Identification and analysis of indicators of Community strengths and outcomes,* Occasional paper No.3., Department of Family and Community Services, Canberra

Bordeaux, P. (1985), 'The forms of capital', in J.G Richardson (ed.), *Handbook of Theory and Research for Sociology of Education,* Greenwood, New York, pp.241-58.

Birrell, B., Healy, E., & Kinnaird, B. (2013). *Australia's Immigration Revolution.* Melbourne University Publishing.

Birrell, B., & McCloskey, D. (2019). Australia's' jobs and growth' strategy: pathway to a low productivity economy.

Brehm, J. M., Eisenhauer, B. W., & Krannich, R. S. (2004). Dimensions of community attachment and their relationship to well-being in the amenity-rich rural west. Rural Sociology, 69(3), 405-429.

Bracht, N. & Tsouros, A. (1990). 'Principles and Strategies of Effective Community Participation', *Health Promotion International,* Vol. 5, No. 3, pp. 199-208

Brown, D. L. (2002). Migration and Community: Social Networks in a Multilevel World. Rural Sociology, 67(1).

Brown, C. 1984, *The Art of Coalition Building:* A Guide for Community leaders, American Jewish Committee, New York

Cooper, R. (2020). *Labour Market Outcomes for Migrants: Evidence and Policy. Economic Record,* 96(315), 110-130.

Cheers, B. Edwards, J & Graham, L. (2004) 'Community strength and health in rural communities', Proceedings of the SA PHC_RED Conferenc, J Fuller (ed.), Adelaide.

Cheers, B. Cock, G. Hilton Keele, L. Kruger & Trigg, H. (2006), 'Measuring community capacity: An electronic auditing tool', in M. Rogers & D. Jones (eds), *The Changing nature of Australia's Country towns,* VURRN Press Ballarat

Coleman, J. (1988), 'Social capital in the creation of human capital', *American Journal of Sociology,* Vol.94, Supplement: s95-s120

Cavaye, J., & Ross, H. (2022). Community resilience and community development: What mutual opportunities arise from interactions between the two concepts? Community Development for Times of Crisis, 75-96.

Cavaye, J. (2000). *The Role of Government in Community Capacity Building,* Department of Primary Industries, Brisbane.

Cooper, R & Foley, M. (2020), Workplace gender equality in the post-pandemic era: Where to next, Journal of Industrial Relations 2021, Vol. 63(4)

Department of Home Affairs. (2021). *Adult Migrant English Program (AMEP)*. Retrieved from Department of Home Affairs.

Dowling, B., Powell, M.,Glendenning, C. (2004) 'Conceptualizing successful partnerships', *Health and Social care in the Community,* Vol. 12, no. 4, pp. 309-17

Dwyer, C. (1999). Contradictions of community: questions of identit for young British Muslim women. Environment and Planning A, 31(1), 53-68.

Flora, J.L. (1998), 'Social capital and communities of place', *Rural Sociology,* Vol.63, no. 4, pp. 481-505.

Fiske, J. (2010). Introduction to communication studies. Routledge.

FECCA. (2022). *Federation of Ethnic Communities' Councils of Australia*. Retrieved from FECCA.

Guterbock, T. (1999). Community of interest: Its definition, measurement, and assessment. Sociological Practice Review. 1(2):88-104.

Gona, J.K., Hartley, S., Newton, J. (2006), 'Using participatory rural appraisal (PRA) in the identification of children with disabilities in rural kilifi, Kenya'. *Rural and Remote Health 6:* <http: rrh.deakin.edu.au>

Hancock, T. (2009). Act Locally: Community-based population health promotion. Ottawa: Senate Sub-Committee on Population Health, Government of Canada.

Hasson, F., Keeney, S., McKenna, H. (2000). 'Research guidance for the Delphi survey technique', *Journal of Advanced Nursing*, Vol. 32, No. 4, pp. 1008-15

Himmelman, A. T. (1996). PART TWO. Creating Collaborative Advantage, 19.

Hollinsworth, D. (2006). Confronting racism in communities: Guidelines and resources for anti-racism training workshops. Centre for Multicultural Pastoral Care, Paddington, QLD and the University of the Sunshine Coast, Queensland.

Hollinsworth, D. (2006). Race and Racism in Australia. (3rd ed.) Thomson Learning Australia. - 67

Hugo, G 2011, 'A significant contribution: The economic, social and civic contributions of first and second generation humanitarian entrant's summary of findings Australian Government: Department of Social Services', https://www.dss.gov.au/

Hugo, G (2014) 'The Economic Contribution of Humanitarian Settlers in Australia', International Migration, vol.52, no.2, pp. 32-52.

Himmelman, A. T. (1996). *Collaboration for a Change: Definitions, Decision-Making, and the Role of Collaboration in Community Development.* Journal of Community Development, 31(4), 33-54.

Hollinsworth, D. (2006). *Cultural Adjustment and Migration: A Comparative Perspective. Australian Journal of Social Issues*, 41(3), 315-332.

Hugo, G. (2011). *Economic Impacts of Immigration. Australian Economic Review*, 44(1), 93-103.

Israel, G., Beaulieu, L. (1990) 'Community Leadership', in A.E. Luloff & L.E. Swanson (eds), *American Rural Communities*, Westview Press, Boulder, Colorado, pp. 181-202

Jupp, J. (2002) From White Australia to Woomera: The Story of Australian Immigration. West Nyack, NY: Cambridge University Press

Kenny, S., Connors, P. (2017). *Developing Communities for the Future* (5th ed.). South Melbourne: Cengage Learning Australia.

Kaufman, H. F. 1959. Toward an interactional conception of community. Social Forces 38(1):8–17.

Markus, A. (2019). *Australia's Socially Diverse Population: Issues and Implications. Australian & New Zealand Journal of Sociology*, 55(4), 518-535.

Mohr, J. (1988). *Networks and Community: The Role of Local Organizations in Social Development*.

MacQueen, K. M., McLellan, E., Metzger, D. S., Kegeles, S., Strauss, R. P., Scotti, R., Blanchard, L., & Trotter, R. T., 2nd (2001). What is community? An evidence-based definition for participatory public health. *American journal of public health*, *91*(12), 1929–1938.

McLean, R. & Stutter, H. (1993), *Advocacy Training in Community Services:* a Training Package for consumers and service providers, TasCOSS/ Tasmania TAFE

Markus, A. & Arnup, J. (2010). Mapping Social Cohesion 2009: The Scanlon Foundations Surveys Full Report (2010), section 12

Melville, B. (1993). 'Rapid rural appraisal: Its role in health planning in developing countries', *Tropical Doctor*, Vol. 23, pp. 55-8

Morris, E. W. (2006). An unexpected minority: White kids in an urban school. Rutgers University Press.

McKinnon, J. (2013). The Environment: A Private Concern or a Professional Practice Issue for Australian Social Workers? *Australian Social Work, 66*(2), 156–170. https://doi.org/10.1080/0312407X.2013.782558

McKinnon, S. L. (2008). Unsettling resettlement: Problematizing "Lost Boys of Sudan" resettlement and identity. Western Journal of Communication, 72(4), 397-414.

Midgley, G., & Ochoa-Arias, A. (Eds.). (2004). Community operational research: OR and systems thinking for community development. Springer Science & Business Media.

Mohr, J. W. (1998). Measuring meaning structures. Annual review of sociology, 24(1), 345-370.

Oakley, P. and Marsden, D. (1982) "Radical community development in the Third World", in Craig, G., Derricourt, N., and Loney, M. (eds.). Community Work and the State, L - 59

Phillips R and Pittman R H (2009) An Introduction to Community Development. Routledge.

Pigg, K. (1999). 'Community Leadership and community theory: A practical synthesis, *Journal of the Community Development Society,* Vol. 30, no. 2, pp. 196-212

Pillai, J. (2022). Cultural Mapping: A Guide to Understanding Place, Community and Continuity (: Revised and Updated). Strategic Information and Research Development Centre.

Pillai, R., Morris, S., & Gupta, H. (2017). *Addressing the Needs of Migrant Communities: A Policy Review. Social Policy Journal of New Zealand,* 60, 55-72.

Portes, A. (1998), "Social Capital: its origins and applications in Modern sociology'. *Annual Review of Sociology,* Vol. 13, pp. 1-24

Putnam, R. D. (2000). Bowling alone: the collapse and revival of American community. New York, Simon & Schuster.

Putnam, R. D. (1993), 'Bowling Alone: America's declining social capital', *Journal of Democracy, vol. 6, pp. 65-78*

Robert Stebbins, Sociology. The Study of Society, Harper and Row: New York, 1987, p. 534).

Rissel, C., Bracht, n. (1999), 'Assessing community needs, resources and readiness', in N.Bracht (ed.) Health Promotion at the Community Level-2-New Advance, Sage Publications Inc., Thousand Oaks, California, pp.59-69 90

Rost, J. (1993). 'Leadership in the new millennium', *The Journal of Leadership Studies,* Vol. 1, no. 1, pp. 92-110

Speckman, M. (2014). Towards an asset-based model: *A critical reflection on student material support with special reference to clienthood/citizenship tension.* Perspectives on student affairs in South Africa, 121.

Sampson, R. J., Raudenbush, S. W., & Earls, F. *(1997). Neighborhoods and violent crime: A multilevel study of collective efficacy. science, 277(5328), 918-924.*

Sharp, J. (2001). Locating the Community Field: A study of interorganizational network structure and capacity for community action. Rural Sociology, 66(3), 403-424.

Stone, C. N. (2000). Civic engagement in American democracy.

Swan, P., & McKinnon, J. (2013). *Access to Services and Support for CALD Communities.* Journal of Australian Social Policy, 52(1), 45-65.

Warren, M. R. (2009). Community Organizing in Britain: The Political Engagement of Faith–Based Social Capital. City & Community, 8(2), 99-127.

Wilkinson, K. (1991). The community in rural America. New York: Greenwood Press.

Wilkinson, K. (1970). 'The community as a social field', *Social Forces*, Vol. 48, pp. 311-22

Zakus, J.D., Lysack, C.L. (1998). Revisiting community participation. Journal of health policy and planning, 13(1), 1-12

www.ingramcontent.com/pod-product-compliance
Lightning Source LLC
Chambersburg PA
CBHW010824070526
44583CB00022B/2927